MENTORING
WOMEN LEADERS

Dream Write Publishing Ltd.
P.O. Box 57083 RPO Eastgate
Sherwood Park AB
T8A 5L7
www. dreamwritepublishing.ca

Mentoring Women Leaders
ISBN # 978-1927510-61-2
Sponsored by Womanition
Cover Design by Shauna Madsen

Library and Archives Canada Cataloging in Publication
Mentoring Women Leaders
Briggs, Dorothy
Edmonton, AB

Printed in the US by CreateSpace

FORWARD

To inaugurate our uplifting compilation, "Mentoring Women Leaders", we sought out the wisdom of a true visionary, one of the foremost authorities on powerful women role models.

A dynamic maverick in her own right, former Global Television Edmonton prime time news anchor, Lesley MacDonald is now the founder, producer and host of "Woman of Vision", an ingenious project showcasing the stories of inspirational women, the challenges they've faced and the successes they celebrate. With twenty-one years to her credit, profiling at least one outstanding woman a month, undoubtedly Lesley speaks from experience when she shares her views on setting priorities, overcoming adversity and the value of strong, positive female mentors in business.

Unique from other little girls growing up, Lesley admits to being a bit of a tomboy, with a forthright assertiveness that likely accounts in part for her rapid career climb at Global Toronto, from copy clerk to associate producer to anchor desk in what was then a noticeably testosterone riddled landscape.

"Most of the women were secretaries and there were no female mentors at first." Lesley muses, "Global hired its first female assignment editor, producer and anchor during the first few years I was there."

The undaunted Ms. MacDonald was clearly adept at independently making her way despite the dearth of relevant role models. So, are mentors necessarily of value for women in business today?

"Definitely!" Lesley affirms emphatically, "Because women feel alone. They think they're the only ones going through it all. They need support systems and inspiration from other women who have walked the path."

A seasoned "coach" in your corner can lead you to accept yourself, to embrace your strengths as well as your weaknesses, and make the most of what you've got, using even supposed "drawbacks" to your advantage. "I just love when people underestimate me," laughs Lesley, a confident, petite blonde. "While they're busy judging my brain by my body size and hair colour, I can get in there and get the job done before the competition even notices!"

Certainly an experienced mentor can help you discover your "Why?" and your "Big Picture", inspiring you to build on the essence of what truly motivates you. Woman of Vision recipients are all in the community, consistently accomplishing the awe inspiring. Yet when asked to sum up their "vision", many hesitate. They don't readily know. Interesting to note that consistent positive feedback includes citing back to that exercise in defining themselves as one of the most powerful outcomes of the WOV experience.

For Lesley, at this point, it really is all about that "Big Picture", making the deliberate decision not to be pulled in all different directions, but focusing instead on specific carefully-discerned priorities and streamlining your time, projects and energies towards those greater goals.

Obviously a savvy game plan, but when you encounter the inevitable setbacks along the way, Lesley urges entrepreneurs to, "Listen to your instincts. They speak volumes."

According to this multi-talented Managing Director, the driving force behind New ViewPoint Communications, you just keep moving forward, viewing any adversity simply as climbing the "ladder of life". At the beginning your destination is not apparent, but you must trust in yourself and have faith that with every obstacle you overcome, you climb another rung on the ladder and, in the process, get to see more of the horizon.

"You never do anything truly great in this world until you've been through incredible challenges."

Clearly Lesley MacDonald, the quintessential Woman of Vision, walks the talk.

ACKNOWLEDGEMENTS

"MENTOR". The word, as defined by the dictionary, refers to "a wise and trusted counselor or teacher, an influential senior sponsor or supporter." But the concept of "mentorship", the significance this special relationship brings to people's lives, the confidence and insight it instills in the protégé, not to mention the knowledge, and the strength, commitment, and courage it demands from the advisor, honestly, attempting to put the depth of all of this into a simple definition, I find mere words just do not suffice at all.

There are as many ways and means to inspire a student as there are teachers out there making a difference, each one delightfully unique in their own lessons. I know you will find encouragement here, advice that resonates with you, and the dreams you have for your business. I think that's why it's so important to me that you have this chance to know a bit more about the authors of these chapters, share a "behind the scenes" look at the mentors behind the stories, thoughtfully hand picked to enhance this book, so you will begin to love and appreciate them as much I do.

First and foremost, I would like to pay tribute to the multi-talented conference speaker and workshop leader, **Alexis Leclair**, author of the insightful new book, "Retirement Grove: Finding Yours". An extraordinary mentorship program manager herself, Alexis certainly plays an integral role in the Womanition Mentorship Program's ongoing success. In fact, had it not been for her generosity in sharing her corporate knowledge, providing the format and processes that still remain the foundation for our program, I am sure the project would not have been so seamlessly launched. Thank you, Alexis! I am profoundly grateful for your support.

A true professional, and one of the most trustworthy people I know, **Donna Worthington** CFP EPC, has excelled as a certified financial planner for over two decades now. Dedicated to the monetary health and well being of her clients, she literally "insists" they become investment savvy for their own good, pointing out their choice of potential futures, carry a Gucci bag or garbage one. Having established a reputation at "Womanition" as the definitive oracle for all things financial, Donna was the perfect choice to come on board at the start of our mentorship program. A superlative speaker, as her rave reviews will attest, her astute advice is showcased regularly in numerous industry magazines.

Chartered accountants and partners, **Ida Colby and Jennifer Steckly**, want theirs to be your "dream" firm, the one that truly puts clients first, treating you so well you'd never hesitate to recommend referrals. They want to be your accounting "ideal", standing head and shoulders above all the rest when it comes to actually delivering on all promises. It's no surprise to me then that these entrepreneurial visionaries own, operate and oversee an accounting organization staffed predominately with **women**! Well, if you want the job done right...

Joanne Kirk FCIP, EPC is a powerful advocate for the financial PLAN, expertly guiding you to put the financial pieces together for a brilliant tomorrow, while still allowing enough flexibility to accomplish your more immediate goals today. Whether working with single individuals, families, or entire corporations, Joanne is committed to providing the practical strategies necessary for all stages of their lives, or business development, even as they extend to the often overlooked areas of tax and retirement planning. A strong believer in building positive longstanding client relationships, for Ms. Kirk, customer service is key!

Many times I have said, "**Shauna Madsen**, you're a genius!" The woman is a veritable font of brilliant ideas! During the five years she designed "Womanition Magazine", the publication won multiple awards for design, advertising, and layout in the special edition category. A master marketing specialist providing creative marketing solutions for her clients' projects from the planning phase right through to development and implementation, Shauna's specialties include branding, customer engagement, and business plan development with visual communications, and that's only scratching the surface. Creativity, ingenuity, flexibility and focus, believe me, Shauna's got what it takes!

Wendy Olson-Brodeur CFP, CFDS, CSC, stands out in the world of financial planners, not just for the holistic practices she "preaches" to ensure the "wealth wellness" of her clients, but because she is one of the very few professionals in Canada to have earned a Financial Divorce Specialist (FDS) designation, qualifying her to wisely steer individuals stressed out by separation and divorce situations away from precipitously making costly financial mistakes that could sabotage their future. Navigating such highly emotional waters at the most troubled of times in people's lives, it certainly doesn't hurt that our Wendy is a trained Mediator as well!

A bookkeeper is one of the most important contractors you'll need in your business, so best hire an outstanding one! Experienced bookkeeping empresario, **Barb Steckly**, designed her firm, Preferred Client Services Group LTD, currently home to a dozen other numbers professionals, with an ingenious business model in mind that allows each bookkeeper therein to set up as an entrepreneur in and of themselves under her business "umbrella". Good thinking, Barb, and that's only the beginning. When you're "bookkeeping with the stars", you learn that your books are so much more than a historical record or a means of determining how much money to send to the government. With the value added reports this innovative firm provides their clients, your mundane records transform into an indispensable financial "compass" of sorts by which you can set the future course for your business.

Expertise in communication is a prime prerequisite for a compelling mentor, and when it comes to effectively conveying relevant information, Accredited Business Communicator and Public Relations Director, **Bernadette Geronazzo** is at the top of her game! A multi linguist, fluent in English, French, Italian, and Spanish, this former television writer and Calgary Herald columnist has used her creative prowess in advertising and corporate communication plans to promote countless client companies, ranging from independently owned businesses right on through to multi-national corporations.

Cheryl Dyck B.comm w/CS Minor, MBA is a Certified Business ActionCOACH with a passion for helping your business succeed and grow, making it possible for entrepreneur owners to have the work life balance they deserve. Focusing on key areas such as customer service, sales, marketing, team building and business development, to name a few, Cheryl encourages her clients to redefine their dreams and vision, implementing the necessary systems, strategies, and tactics that allow their business ventures to thrive.

Fired at fifty, **Christine Till**, unlike other women of a "certain age", did not give up, or give in! Reinventing herself instead as an enthusiastic social media aficionado, whimsically dubbed the "Marketing Mentress", she has now claimed LinkedIn as her professional playground, making more and more business contacts on a daily basis. As a participant in her exclusive hands-on workshops or personal coaching sessions, you can learn yourself, from the ground up, how to utilize LinkedIN to build your own valuable business relationships that will ultimately bring you more sales.

Accomplished marketing, media and public relations professional, **Donna McColl**, is committed to getting your message out to the right people, in the right way, at the right time. Formerly a communications manager in the public sector, Donna has extensive experience in motivating staff to explore their full potential, a valuable advantage she brings to her mentorship role. Having opted now for the entrepreneurial life, she provides consulting and writing services to an array of clients, from sole proprietors right to internationally high tech organizations.

Self-proclaimed "serial entrepreneur", **Mary Lou Gutscher**, has built profitable businesses in retail, telemarketing and publishing, where she achieved millions in annual sales. Having traveled the path herself, Mary Lou is now an empathetic advocate for emerging women entrepreneurs, and through her company, "Magnetic Business Solutions", she currently devotes her prodigious energies to guiding others to grow their businesses profitably. A positive, caring coach, Mary Lou is also a popular emcee and much sought after conference speaker, but her true legacy as a mentor will be the lucky ones whose lives she has changed and "saved", who are now eager to follow in her footsteps.

Anyone would love to know what **Rita-anne Fuss** knows about the network marketing business! A bonafide sales dynamo, she has taken her delight in fabulous fashion jewellery and built it into an incredible, award winning empire, and this girl has the trophy cabinets full of top sales recognition awards to prove it, not to mention all those amazing memories from all those amazing reward trips all over the world! Partnering in the business with her husband, Curtis, this charismatic self-starter has spent the last 27 years bringing the joy of Fifth Avenue Jewelry Collection into the homes of countless women across Canada, while, at the same time, expertly empowering her extensive sales team in the best ways to achieve their potential. "ASK! ASK! ASK!" is her famous motto. Yes, just ask, because if you don't, how will you ever get the sale?

Award winning author and motivational humorist, **Zandra Bell**, is well known on the corporate conference scene for creating original, intelligent humour designed to inspire and enhance human potential. Performed in the guise of her comedic alter ego, the iconic "Shirley Best", Zandra's innovative key notes, specifically researched, and completely customized according to clients' business objectives are the ultimate solution to resolving workplace stress, and raising staff morale and productivity. In her role as a business revitalization mentor, Zandra ingeniously combines her marketing savvy, comedic gifts, and creative public speaking and wordsmithing talents to inspire entrepreneurs to dream BIG and invent their own innovative "empires". I just know when you meet the unique Ms. Bell you'll simply fall in love with her brilliant writing!

Cyndy Morin's conviction that effective and affordable access to justice be available to all members of the community no matter what their specific circumstances ultimately led her to establish the "Resolve Legal Group" a team of family law experts committed to strategizing the best solution to meet your specific legal needs in the most efficient and cost effectual way possible. A "wonder woman" of many talents and far reaching interests, including a passion for aviation and a foray into private investigation, Cyndy also teaches college level family law courses in conjunction with the Alberta Law Foundation. For a high flying amateur pilot like Ms. Morin, apparently not even the sky is the limit. Our Cyndy goes above and beyond!

Darlene Schindel, a trained RN herself, became the "Nurse's Nurse" in response to a need she recognized in the healthcare community itself for high level holistic support of the healthcare professionals who work within. Her vision is to transform healthcare from the inside out, to support and inspire its professionals, one by one, to lead where they stand, and be the change they KNOW and WANT to see. An innovative transformational leadership coach with hands on experience in front line neuro-nursing, she stands for integrity, communication, and building strong relationships based on shared values and trust.

As a devoted life-long learner, **Deborah Kurach** is a shining example of career longevity, commitment and high standards in life and in business. Owner operator of one of the finest salon spas in Alberta, she is not only dedicated to providing ongoing education and mentoring to her staff of over twenty-five professionals, but this avid philanthropist is very focused on generously giving back to the community, supporting friends, clients, and numerous charities. Certainly Deborah is, as they say, a "real class act."

Ralph Waldo Emerson claimed, "Life is a journey, not a destination", and holistic life coach, **Deborah Nichol**, owner of "Healing Heart Wellness" would not only heartily agree with him, but she would encourage you to savour every beautiful, messy moment of that journey and appreciate the scenery along the way, otherwise you'll miss the whole wonderful thing! Deborah is all about helping people to live an authentic life embracing every aspect of their true selves, weaknesses and flaws inclusive. Instead of wasting energy trying to mask doubts and insecurities, recognize them instead as an integral part of knowing who you really are. You are "enough" right now.

The conceptual roots of the Enneagram Personality Theory began in the Middle East dating back two thousand years. While it is a system with both psychological and spiritual components, the compassionate and intuitive, **DK Beitel**, relies on her own insightful observations and self-reflection as well, in her personal consulting and eye-opening workshops designed to increase our understanding as to what motivates others' behaviour. Certainly this caring and knowledgeable professional is doing her part to make the world a much more peaceful and harmonious place.

A committed crusader for enhanced education and the widespread awareness of Type 1 diabetes, **Eva Shaw** Ph.D. is a registered clinical counselor experienced in helping the affected and their families contend with the many tumultuous issues associated with the disease, from workplace stress, anxiety, depression, low self esteem to communication and relationship breakdowns. As a passionate advocate for overall societal reforms as well, in the areas of family violence, human trafficking and homelessness, Eva definitely walks her talk. Clearly she has not let her own experience of living for over fifty years with diabetes herself stop her from making a positive difference.

"Uplift Expert", author **Lil Lezarre**, uplifts your life in more ways than one, in her varying roles as an accomplished L.T. D. "Living Through Divorce" Transition Guide, certified meditation instructor, and proud owner of a women's intimate apparel company, fondly known as "Tender Loving Cups". A veritable go-getter, full of boundless energy, Lil credits her own personal mentors as being instrumental in keeping her focused and forward thinking. Once she took that leap of faith in her abilities and opened her own company, she has never looked back. Not bad for a woman who started out as one of the protégés in our first Mentorship Program and has now been selected as a mentor herself! I have seen huge growth on her part, and admire her strength and fortitude in doing it "her way"

Pam McCormack our "Irish babe", is a confident, gregarious, avidly enthusiastic supporter of all women in business. Longtime owner of a successful exclusive day spa, specializing in an array of physically relaxing, as well as spiritually affirming holistic treatments, Pam lights up the world with that famous Irish flair and fabulous sense of humor, proudly crediting her husband for her success at every turn, in his role as "the backbone" of her company.

Sam Rafoss RHN is a trained social worker, holistic nutritionist and reiki master, but now, as an award winning business coach, she's following a higher calling. Yes, after many years of front line caregiving she decided to step back, and, in her new role as a business strategist for holistic and nutrition practices, she now gives "care" to the front line caregivers! Well, certainly someone has to help the healers replenish their energies, and our Sam has the knowledge and the expertise to do just that, using her marketing skills to help health & wellness practitioners determine their niche and attract their ideal clients, essentially aligning the "corporate" side of their business, so they can concentrate on caring for their clients while making money doing what they love.

Confronted with a negative situation in her past professional life, mortgage expert extraordinaire, **Sandra Fisher**, could have let it bring her down, but, instead, she had the foresight and the courage to use it as a catalyst to move her forward, and after a quarter century of reporting to someone else, she opened her own brokerage firm, Verico iMortgage Solutions. As a mentor, Sandra has a reputation for putting others at ease acting as a practical sounding board. A life long learner herself, she is committed to the ongoing training and education of her team of twenty specialists, and will search inexhaustibly to find the perfect solution for her clients. A brilliant addition to our "Womanition" mentorship team, her story will motivate and inspire.

Shirley Borrelli leads by example. As an accomplished business strategist, award winning image consultant, and C.O.N.F.I.D.E.N.C.E. coach, her services are much sought after in entrepreneurial and corporate circles alike. My clever co-host for our "Womanition" BizBrigade Leadership Conference, Shirley is a beautiful and brilliant collaborator, and a talented mentor. Her early career as an educator is now reflected in her passion for teaching others to fulfill their true potential and bring their business to new levels. Shine on, Shirley!

And you, brilliant Reader, please read on...

MENTORING
WOMEN LEADERS

TOC
Table of Contents

MENTORING
WOMEN LEADERS

DOROTHY BRIGGS

Dorothy Briggs is a name synonymous with the power behind women mentoring women. A driving force in the Albertan business community, this vibrant, dynamic leader has become an undeniable catalyst for women effectively connecting, and collaborating for the greater good.

Gifted with an ardent entrepreneurial spirit, Dorothy has received endless accolades for her accomplishments as the founder and publisher of Womanition® Magazine, a venture so successful that it quickly led to an entire network of Womanition Connect Groups throughout the province uplifting and empowering women in countless communities.

Pursuing her passion, the indomitable Ms. Briggs continues to educate, motivate, and inspire business women, honing the talents of the up and coming through the thriving Womanition Mentorship Program, and the Womanition "BizBrigade" Leadership Conference, rightfully honouring their achievements as well, through her latest project, the innovative Womanition SuPEARLative Awards.

All in all, there is no doubt. Dorothy Briggs is making a difference.

The Power of Irrational Optimism

"No one can succeed without one essential ingredient. There is one trait every successful person possesses: Irrational optimism."

Love at first sight, or should I say, understanding. That's how I felt when I inadvertently came across this phrase one day. I absolutely ADORED it! It completely resonated with me, because I realized in a flash that "irrational optimism" was exactly the driving force behind how I had lived my life to date, and how, having now seen it validated for me right there in writing, I intend to go on living it.

Success requires belief, faith in one's abilities to achieve desired goals. Right from the beginning I knew I had that kind of entrepreneurial spirit, that independent "Well then I'll go out and do it myself!" determination that would shape my career path, and ultimately my whole life. I was the different one among friends and family. My single working mother could barely afford to feed the family, so naturally when, as a young teen, I had to have those "oh so perfect" shoes, I was told a resounding "NO". Ah, even then, when it came to something I wanted, that word "no" was just not in my vocabulary. I had to tackle three jobs, shampooing hair, waiting tables, and scooping ice cream, but I did buy those shoes!

"Unrelenting optimism", the unshakeable conviction that I was going to accomplish what I set my mind to do, despite all the odds stacked against me, that's about the only thing that gave me hope for my future, growing up in a middle class, blue collar family, daughter of a violent, mentally ill, alcoholic father, and then "stay at home" mom. I spent my childhood in frequent terror of my drunken father's physical abuse. No one was safe from his anger or his fists. I recall watching in horror one night as he broke my mother's finger. Those were dark times.

Thankfully, by my early adolescence, my father had abandoned us. As a family, finally we were able to collectively sigh with relief and stop walking on those proverbial eggshells, but now, sadly, the survival of all six of us was all up to my exhausted mom. Looking back, I know I must have learned about inner pride and strong work ethic from my mother, watching her pass up welfare benefits, and take on two jobs instead. Somehow we scraped by, often making do between pay cheques fine dining on raw potatoes and mustard sandwiches.

In fact, one day I took pride too far myself when I refused a charitable donation of a Christmas gift basket at the door. My mother flew out after that basket like it was a crock of gold, which from her perspective, as sole breadwinner, it certainly was. How could I have been so shortsighted? I was just so fiercely self-sufficient for most of my young adult life until I learned that accepting help from others is not at all the weakness I had originally thought, when my views were coloured with the shame of being poor.

I understand much better now that refusing outside help essentially obstructs the flow of abundance pouring in from the universe, abundance that is your birthright. Acceptance, opening up to the "gifts" being given to you freely affirms your belief in your own self-worth, and sets the scene for more prosperity to follow. It took me a very long time to learn that lesson.

I was young and ambitious, bold and beautiful, full of my own power, so headstrong and, of course, I knew everything! I left school early on. After all, what could they teach me? I was in love, so, naturally I would have the whole wedding extravaganza, and I would organize it all, and, of course, pay for it all myself. It didn't even occur to me there was an alternative. I married young, and divorced not that much older. Huge surprise.

If my romantic relationships were not as successful as I would have wished, my career aspirations, at least, were something I could control and direct myself. As a dedicated self-starter, eager to embrace appealing, potentially lucrative opportunities, I worked in many different businesses over the years. Determined to start a carpet cleaning company at one point, I recall approaching the bank for a loan. I was told by some misogynist manager that I was not a good risk for the money because carpet cleaning was a "man's job".

When a television news show focusing on discrimination against women in the business world came to my attention, I contacted them with my story. The day after my segment aired, I was granted the loan. I had it paid back in two months. Man's job! Poor risk! Hmmph! You better not mess with Dorothy Briggs! That was my attitude. I was bound and determined that I was going to make something magnificent of myself, and rue to anyone who got in the way.

Life as a carpeting cleaning queen proved prosperous, but, once I had everything working effectively, it ceased to challenge my restless mind. I was always voraciously searching for something new to learn, and do, and certainly my work as a realtor opened up a whole new avenue for my talents. I'd found my true calling, sales!

Convincing people to listen and take my advice, and then assertively closing the deal, this was child's play for a woman with my dynamic street smarts and persuasive, commanding personality. I was frequently the top salesperson in my branch, as well as the overall company. Of course, I was still convinced I knew "everything" and therefore really didn't ask advice from the veterans. Unaware that the month of December was traditionally the slowest, I continually brought in the highest sales volume at that time of year.

It's so strong, the power of the mind, thus the negative effect buying in to limiting beliefs like this can have on your business success. As I say, I was ignorant of the fact you weren't "supposed" to bring in top sales in December, so I did, proving that it wasn't true at all, just something other less productive realtors used as an excuse when they became discouraged. So often, we entrepreneurs allow the constraints and insecurities of those who influence us to hold us back from pursuing our goals, sometimes even unknowingly.

"You can't do that. A woman can't own a carpet cleaning company."
"You can't make money in the summer. Everyone is on vacation."
"Aren't you a little too old to go back to school?"

There are endless examples of friends and relatives trying to clip our wings and put a stop to our highflying hopes and dreams, not because they're necessarily mean and nasty. In fact, usually it's the opposite. They love us, so, operating unconsciously under their own fears and restrictive core beliefs, they're doing their best to protect us from disappointment and failure.

Here's where the need for "irrational optimism" comes in. We tend to mindlessly accept these statements as solid truths that are carved in stone, but they are just mere thoughts and opinions with no more basis in truth than we choose to give them. To really achieve the amazing life you've imagined, you have to be prepared to think in a way others could consider "irrational" because you're not following all of society's "rules" designed to keep you in line.

You need optimism, that persistently positive mindset that carries you toward your goals, despite the roadblocks the "rational" out there try to throw in your way. If you continue to believe something is true, then, yes, you make it **your** reality. But it doesn't have to be **the** one and only reality. A belief is just a thought that you keep thinking. Think another thought, and you create another reality, your OWN reality, the way you want it to be.

After numerous and varied adventures that took me all across western Canada, finally I decided it was time for me to create a decisively new reality for myself. Naturally, I still wanted to be financially viable, yet maintain a better work life balance. My expertise in sales was making my management team rich. Why couldn't I do all this just for myself? I was ready for a career where I would be the one in sole control.

Along the way, experimenting with various sales professions as I was, I happened to purchase a health and wellness magazine, which I published for almost five years, eventually selling it back to the original owners for 1100% of the original value I'd paid. During my time as a publisher, I had an idea for another magazine theme that scored very well in the test market, especially in my target female demographic. I thought it would be incredible, as well as constructive, to create a magazine about women power in the business realm, a publication that would focus on promoting and, essentially, mentoring women. Thus, my now successfully established and ever expanding brand "Womanition" was born!

It should have been a momentous experience, the debut of my first edition, another glorious coup for the unshakeable Dorothy Briggs. Instead it was one of the most traumatic disasters of my business life! I thought I had effectively communicated my vision for the new magazine to those who had signed on as the entrepreneurs I would showcase. Apparently not. Evidently there was a communication gap, which was subsequently turned into a veritable Grand Canyon by the end of the fiasco.

To this day the exact cause of their dissatisfaction isn't completely clear to me, but, led by one particularly "fiery", outspoken woman, the group verbally attacked me, tearing apart my precious project, and labeling my beloved dream magazine as a "low class catalogue", and "a lousy brochure" among other insults. I was even called out because my innovative brand to express woman power on the move, "Womanition", wasn't a real word!

Heaven forbid I should step out of line and do something different and creative.

It was appalling, and so disillusioning, because this kind of childish school yard behaviour dividing women, setting them against each other is exactly what has traditionally held women back in the business world. My vision was, and still very much is, to show that business women are way above and beyond this unenlightened corporate "cat fighting". I want "Womanition" and everything the brand now stands for, from the magazine to the monthly networking groups, from the mentoring program to the BizBrigade, to unite and empower women so we can collaborate, sustain, and mutually support one another as we advance…and eventually take over the world!!! Okay, let's stop at "advance". Sometimes, while thinking of the amazing "family" of women I have on board today, my heart swells with pride and I get a little carried away.

Disappointed, and disenchanted as I was, you can imagine just what kind of gumption it took to pull myself together enough to publish the second edition. My normally unassailable confidence more than a little deflated, what I really wanted to do was bury my head under the covers and cry. I wasn't about to submit to defeat though, and looking back from my current perspective as the proud publisher of that same "lousy low class catalogue" which has somehow managed to win a trophy case of gold and platinum awards for production, design, layout, special edition and advertising, I will say I'm very glad I banished all my self doubts and despair, and used that horrific incident to spur me on, not stop me in my tracks. That unhappy business woman has since apologized to me in writing for her actions, so I like to think, in retrospect, the whole sordid scenario served as a catalyst for something better for her as well.

It must have been that old irrational optimism kicking in again though, when I not only continued undaunted with my "Womantion" magazine, but eventually began a new venture, "Vavasaur Magazine" a similar publication, profiling male entrepreneurs in the community, which successfully ran for four brilliant years before I made the decision, as a "solopreneur" to focus my energies more on helping business women. Still a third, "Divorce Magazine", is now up and coming, gaining momentum at this point, its purpose to serve as a succinct source of emotional and practical support for those individuals in the process of dissolving their marriage.

The "Womanition" name has continued to rapidly expand. In the last five years alone we have come so far, starting with the creation of the "Womanition Connect Groups", thriving business networking communities, having initially started in Edmonton, are quickly increasing in number, springing up in several other locations — Leduc, Parkland County, Sherwood Park, and Calgary, to date.

The year 2012 marked the first of what is now known as our bi-annual "Womanition BizBrigade Leadership Conference", an educational and motivational experience for women, featuring relevant speakers from various professions focusing on topics related to the themes of "Plan Your Business - Grow Your Business - Grow Yourself". The participant feedback on this event's overall effectiveness has just been tremendous!

With so many of our Womanition enthusiasts now thriving, reaching new heights in their businesses, thanks to all we have to offer, I recently created the "Womanition SuPEARLative Awards Program", a gala luncheon ceremony to honour, not just my amazing "wonder women", but their worthy counterparts representing women in the workforce from all over Alberta, as well. As an inventive twist on the typical awards trophy, our winners are awarded a stunning piece of pearl jewelry to commemorate their outstanding achievements.

That same year, our "Womanition Mentorship Program" was introduced, matching eager protégés with the willing mentor who most closely shares their vision and can best suit their needs as they relate to Marketing and Sales, Finance and Accounting, Image and Branding, Leadership and Development, and Referral Building and Relationships. The response to this venture has been simply overwhelming, with no end to the business leaders offering their expertise and the mentorees ready to receive their guidance.

As for myself, I will say the "Womanition" brand, my little entrepreneurial empire that I have built to give back to the world of women entrepreneurs, truthfully, it's only just begun. The ebb and flow of business being what it is I have always been one to reinvent myself, to seek out new opportunities, but within the "Womanition" realm I have found my true passion, helping women in business to help each other.

I couldn't be more thrilled to work with the ingenious outside consultants and contractors that I do, all top notch experts in their field, and my stellar advisory board, all of us aligned in our vision, our commitment, and our quest for excellence. I have come to rely so much on their professionalism and opinions, because contrary to my earlier conviction, I apparently do not know EVERYTHING, although, I'll admit I have learned a lot.

In my unenlightened days, the concept of "mentoring" was lost on me. I would never tell anyone what I was thinking or planning, nor would I ever dream of asking for advice. I certainly wouldn't give out any helpful information either. I was always sure someone would steal my ideas and take the credit, and then what about me?

I was unknowingly coming from that same place of scarcity that little Dorothy knew only too well as a child. This is such a common misconception that there's only so much to go around in the world so we have to grab all we can at the expense of someone else, whereas the truth is abundance is limitless, and its endless flow is only stimulated, not stymied by the give and take of collaboration. Paying it forward, doesn't diminish what you have but ultimately increases your rewards.

I live to make a difference for women in business and if I can change one reader's life for the better out there, then this little book has done its job. Far from being my swan song, I see this "Mentoring Women Leaders" collection, showcasing some of the best business talents I know, as yet another avenue to reach out to even more women in the world, potential business leaders in their own right, who will hopefully read the stories of the unique individuals within, and come away feeling empowered by all they've accomplished in the face of incredible adversity, inspired to learn from their experiences, to put some of their advice, their hard won wisdom to use in their own lives, and above all, feeling "irrationally optimistic", focused positively and unwaveringly on their goals, secure in the knowledge that they are not alone out there in their business struggles and successes, because we "Womanition" women are here for them, and we care.

You have only to reach out, and we will be there.

Reflections

1.
Have you ever had a loved one, or someone you considered a friend and ally try to discourage you from pursuing a project, or plan of action, even though they knew you were enthusiastic about it, and totally confident in its ultimate success? Who was it? What did you do?

2.
Have you given any thought to other innovative avenues of income you could possibly develop, in keeping with your current knowledge and expertise, which would fit in under your overall "brand"?

3.
Can you pinpoint any setbacks, traumatic events or "failures" in your life that were devastating at the time, but, in retrospect, actually served as catalysts to push you into making a positive change?

4.
When self-doubt overwhelms you, do you have a trusted mentor or confidante who is able to talk with you, point out different perspectives, and help you see the big picture?

5.
It's important to check in on a regular basis and see where your business stands from all aspects. I recommend everyone do a SWOT analysis every year. From a business standpoint, what are your strengths, weaknesses, opportunities, and threats?

6.
Do you think you have "Irrational Optimism"? Where have you seen it in action in your life?

MENTORING
WOMEN LEADERS

Plan Your Business

Donna Worthington, CFP®, EPC

Jennifer Steckly, CA

Joanne Kirk, FCIP, EPC

Shauna Madsen

Wendy Olson-Brodeur,CFDS, CFP, CSC,Mediator

Donna Worthington, CFP®, EPC

Certified Financial Planner
INVESTMENT PLANNING COUNSEL

Donna's first vocation was as a registered nurse. Transitioning into financial services, her second career for more than the last twenty years has been as a professional independent financial planner.

She aspires to educate the public about ethically appropriate financial planning, differentiating her service from just the sale of financial products. Secondly, Donna diligently encourages more women to become financial planners.

Donna has served on many professional boards including twelve years on the National Board of Directors for the Canadian Institute of Financial Planners.

As a frequently sought after speaker she has spoken at local, provincial, and national conferences.

Donna is also a recipient of the YWCA Women of Distinction Award and received the highest marks award in the CFP® program at Grant MacEwan University in Edmonton.

Financial Finesse for Women in Business

Donna Worthington, , CFP®, EPC

On Being a Business Woman

Being an independent business woman offers excitement, challenge, and a more flexible lifestyle. Sharing acquired knowledge, while supporting other business women in their careers, is fundamental to my character and daily "best business practices."

My article will include:

- The Value of Education
- The Need for Networking
- How to Market to Women
- The 3 M's of Marketing (Rush, 2013)
- Sales – The Three Components
- Client Appreciation
- The Business Cycles
- The Need for an Advisory Group
- The Power of Collaboration
- The 3 Traits of Highly Successful People
- A list of suggested books and websites I found valuable

The Value of Education

In financial services I am required to maintain licencing, designations and a minimum of 30 hours of pre-approved courses each year. Such standards are worthy. They validate my professional integrity and communicate client trust.

Your vocational calling may not have this continuing educational requirement! If that's the case, why not "self-improve through regular education up-grading?" Be the best you can be for yourself and the service you provide to others. This especially applies to "baby boomers" who want to start their own businesses for monetary, social or self-fulfillment reasons. Increasing your education will demonstrate your credibility as you join the new wave of entrepreneurs.

---

[1] Callan Rush, Wealth Through Workshops

The Need for Networking

All commerce has a common need - attract new business. Accomplishing this through networking groups is very effective. Why is this? It's the most personal method, within a congenial framework, of introducing yourself to new people and interacting with them.

My networking approach is to spend time with three or four people from a group. I focus on listening and learning about their business, their dreams and challenges. They soon realize my genuine interest and will likely ask for my business card. Before giving it to them, I write a brief summary of what we discussed on the back of my card. I then ask for their card. Never just "work a room" handing out your business cards! Change up the groups you belong to and record where leads originate. Most importantly, take your time and be sincere.

How to Market to Women

Callan Rush, in her many seminars (I paraphrase), said "effective marketing to women should be accomplished in small groups, through education where you solve their real world problems."

I have provided financial services to many remarkable women. Many are referrals, some have heard me speak, and others have read my articles in women's magazines.

In the first appointment with me, I ask them: "How did you come to make this appointment?" They say: "You sounded credible, confident and genuine." It became very clear that having small events for "women only" with well-selected speakers who attendees could relate to, brought credibility to me and comfort to them. This gave birth to my event, Ladies Day Out. In collaboration with other professionals, I provide a reassuring forum of education, empowerment, and entertainment.

When meeting with families, I always ask: "What is your greatest need that could be solved through proper financial planning?" I always try to solve their immediate needs first and then complete a comprehensive financial plan. This demonstrates that I listen, educate, and develop a plan that is realistically attainable through specific goal setting. My findings are usually that women want to be educated in financial planning — they genuinely appreciate my efforts and feel comfortable sending referrals.

The 3 M's of Marketing

The 3M's of marketing are: "Magnetize, Mesmerize, and Monetize". These are pure concepts, which only function in the order shown. Change the sequence, it just doesn't work!

To *"magnetize"* is to *"draw people to you."* How might you do that? First of all, you have to show up and be genuinely engaged with the people you meet. Be a sincerely charitable person first, i.e. one who is giving without any expectation of receiving.

For my events, I pay all the expenses. There is no registration fee.

I invite a charity representative (for example a woman's shelter) to speak for 5 minutes. During the event, attendees are encouraged to support the charity by contributing spare cash or cheques into a paper bag on their table. I match these donations. Before the event closes, the final dollar amount is announced. Concluding an event philanthropically is positive. Over the years, we've given thousands of dollars to charities.

Always have a beautiful door prize (my speakers follow this as well). My draw slip has a call to action such as, *"Would you like to meet with me for a complimentary needs analysis of your financial position?"* I only contact the ones who answer "yes". Of those, the majority I do meet with will likely become clients. When we meet, they recognise my ability to sustain them through my process, products, and expertize. In essence, this is the *"mesmerize"* stage. The outcome is that the client now has a financial plan and I am fairly compensated from the insurance or investment companies I used to solve their financial issues.

Staying in business requires money, but not at any cost! Be ethical, honest, and clear in your marketing plan.

Sales - The Three Components

This is one of my favourite topics. When I first came into the financial field, people would say *"that's a far stretch from nursing."* My answer: *"It's the same process, just different products."* Whatever your career field, there are three components: people, products, and process.

---

[1] Callan Rush, Wealth Through Workshops

Individual personal needs may differ but, generically, most people are similar. The aspect that truly changed for me was the product from health care to financial services. I transposed the nursing process from caring and goals-based to financial planning terms.

The greatest difference between you and your competitors is your process. My process has three well-defined meetings.

The first meeting I call "*discovery*". I meet with the prospective client and determine what they need in a financial advisor. I explain what I offer to my clients and what I expect from my clients. If we both feel it's a good fit, we set a date for appointment #2.

At the second meeting, we review their goals, existing financial status, pensions, RRSPs, RESPs, etc., and then I set a date for the final meeting.

Between meeting #2 and #3, I structure and complete a personal written client plan.

Appointment #3 is a review of their plan, which they take home. Sometimes a 4th appointment is required to review newly emerging issues.

Client Appreciation

Ensuring your clients know how much you appreciate them is important. I demonstrate that recognition by telling them I value their confidence in me. As well, I host client events, using an attractive written and mailed invitation that expresses "Sure hope you can make it."

Events have included stage, theatre, sports, science, educational seminars, and speciality dinners, to name a few.

The Business Cycles

My marketing expert, George Hartman in his book, Blunder Wonder Thunder advises: "*You must accept the 'irony of success' - what got you where you are won't keep you where you are.*" [3] He suggests that every 3 to 5 years you need to re-invent a part of your business. "Even more important, you need the foresight and courage to make changes even when it is not yet obvious that change is necessary." [4]

[3] George Hartman: Blunder, Wonder, Thunder., 7.
[4] Ibid., 7.

Although his book is directed to financial advisors, concepts he presents are applicable to other vocations and the chapter is worth a look.

- *The Blunder stage --- which marks the first twelve to twenty-four months you are an advisor --- is a high-action period of making mistakes and learning lessons. Client relationships are based on filling simple needs using a few products you know and trust; you have few systems in place, so inefficiency is built into your practice. Your personality and energy drives your progress. The good news: provided the mistakes you make aren't terminal, you survive.*

- *The Wonder stage dawns as the enthusiasm and energy of the Blunder stage wanes. During this six-to twelve-month period. You ask: "I wonder if this is all worth it?" If you answer, "No, it isn't worth it," you will leave the business. If you answer, "Yes, this business is definitely worth it," you will add a caveat: "If I am going to survive, prosper and enjoy this, I have to do things differently." So, you hire your first assistant --- to free you to implement your revised strategy. "Planning" becomes the primary basis for client relationships, supported by simple systems.*

- *If you ask the right question during the Wonder period --- and respond appropriately --- your business accelerates with a velocity beyond expectation. In this Thunder era (which can last many years), more and more of your business comes from existing clients and referrals.*[5]

The Need for an Advisory Group

Who do you go to if you have a question? Ideally, it's a person you can trust and confide in who will offer constructive criticism and feedback.

My advisory council changes from year to year as I meet more successful people. One of my best friends and entrepreneur always says: "*You are the average of the five people you spend the most time with.*" Choose your advisory council carefully — positive people who are supportive. My council consists of: an accountant, a marketing expert, a successful real estate agent, a mortgage broker, a business coach, and others who can help me succeed.

[5] Ibid., 7.

Twice a year, I sponsor lunch in a private dining room of a well-known restaurant. We introduce ourselves to the group. Individually, we state what we do, what worked to improve our business in the past year, and, equally important, what we should stop doing. Utilizing the concepts of *"blunder, wonder, thunder"* everyone shares and learns new ideas that could work for their business.

The Power of Collaboration

If there is one thing that says "*that grew my business the most*," it is by far collaborating with other professionals!

My example within my process is Ladies Day Out. This is a full day event including lunch for all. We have 100 plus ladies who attend to listen to excellent speakers. The event's emphasis is to educate, empower, and entertain.

Collaboratively, each speaker is required to invite 10 ladies to the event. Many speakers use it as their own client appreciation for their top 10 clients, as there isn't any cost to attend.

Let's do the math: 7 speakers X 10 guests equals 70 new people who I am in front of. I actually get 30 or 40 women (my client appreciation); they bring a friend — a great referral building program.

Outcome: I meet 70 new people. My guest speakers meet 90 - 120 new people. This is what I call a 3-way-win product. Each speaker has a display table with a draw valued at $50.00 that must reflect a prize of immediate gratification (wine, chocolates etc.). Their draw slips have a call to action. The ladies are assured they will only receive a follow-up call if they give their permission on the draw slip. This becomes the "*call to action*."

It's a wonderful fulfilling event for speakers and attendees. Regularly I've heard, "please, invite me next year."

The following year, you move forward with new speakers, new guests, new prospects — new clients. Collaboration with other professionals draws your business to new heights.

The Three Traits of Highly Successful People

In their book, *The Triple Package*, authors Amy Chua and Jed Rubenfeld illustrate how three unlikely traits (superiority + insecurity + impulse control) explain the rise and fall of cultural groups in America. I recommend it as a great read.

Are these not some of the same traits required to be a successful entrepreneur?

Superiority: We need to believe we are not only good at our profession but, perhaps, the best at it. If we don't have confidence in ourselves, who will?

Insecurity: Have you ever awakened in the middle of the night thinking that what you have accomplished is about to crash and burn? Is it all worth it? Every entrepreneur has, although many will not admit it.

Impulse Control: How often does something shiny get our attention? It would be so easy to follow the crowd! Stand back, make an informed decision about options and then be prepared to live with them.

Remember, people want to do business with people who look and sound confident. Learn from other successful people. I highly recommend the suggested books and websites below. They've helped me and, when you digest them and take action, you'll find them helpful, too.

The List of Books and Websites

1. Chua Amy and Rubenfeld Jed, *The Triple Package*: *How three unlikely traits explain the rise and fall of cultural groups in America* (Penquin Press New York NY, 2014) Website: www.thepenquinpress.com

2. Hartman George with Wilmott Tessa, *Blunder Wonder Thunder*: *Powering your practice to new heights* (Market Logics Inc., Toronto ON, 2010) Website: www.info@marketlogics.ca

3. Rush Callan, *Wealth Through Workshops*: *Your step-by-step guide to a life-changing, lucrative workshop, retreat or seminar business* (Leader to Luminary Training, 2013) Website: www.leadertoluminary.com

Reflections

1.
Continuing education validates your professional integrity and communicates client trust.

2.
Networking should be genuine and credible.
Network, Network, Network.

3.
Market to women in small groups utilizing: education, empowerment, and entertainment.

4.
Have an ethical well-defined business process.
Demonstrate honest client appreciation.

5.
Regularly analyze your business cycle process.

6.
Have a credible advisory group.

7.
Work collaboratively with other trustworthy professionals and charities.

8.
Learn from those who excel at their profession.

Testimonials

"Donna combines an incredible knowledge of the financial world with a caring, giving personality. She is interested in my well-being and always acts in my best interests. She is always available to her clients."

Lorraine Hupka,
THE original basket boutique

"Donna has been our financial planner for several years ... we have found her to be extremely knowledgeable, trustworthy, ethical, and professional. Donna's advice has been most beneficial to us personally and, as well, for our business."

Charmaine Hammond, MA, BA
Professional Speaker, Award Winning Author

"With her credentials, she is imminently capable to find the right product and investment strategy totally suited to my age and stage in life and then to match it to my concerns of risk. I wouldn't hesitate to recommend Donna Worthington to any person who is looking to plan a sound financial future.

Margret McGee
Teacher, ECBS (retired)

Please contact Donna for information on upcoming seminars, workshops or speaking engagements.

Donna Worthington, *CFP®, EPC*
Investment Planning Counsel
Certified Financial Planner
Tel: 780-702-1551
Email: dworthington@ipcc.org

MENTORING
WOMEN LEADERS

Jennifer Steckly, CA

Raised by two entrepreneurial parents, Jennifer Steckly learned from an early age to live and breathe business. With a talent for speed and accuracy with numbers, she worked in her mother's bookkeeping business from the age of 12.

That path led to her Chartered Accountant designation in 2011. In 2013, she and her business partner, Ida Colby formed Colby•Steckly Chartered Accountants Ltd. Known for her ability to successfully tackle complex files, Jennifer's financial insights and advice help her clients prosper. Away from work, Jennifer has a passion for physical fitness and a love of theatre and live music.

Three Keys to Financial Mentorship

Jennifer Steckly, CA

Both my parents were entrepreneurs in our house when I was growing up, so I had the benefit of their mentoring regarding the world of business. I learned really young about setting goals and achieving them. Because I had a passion for numbers from the time I learned to count, my mother showed me how to help her in her bookkeeping business when I was just a teenager.

That passion for numbers and my flair for business pulled me through university to the fulfillment of my dream in 2013 of starting a chartered accounting firm. Now, I and my business partner, Ida Colby, have the distinct privilege of mentoring other business women in the achievement of their business dreams.

While being in business isn't just about the numbers, your numbers will be a deciding factor in almost every decision you make. My dad always says that if a business won't work on paper, then it won't work in real life. Over and over I have found this to be true. So when a client comes to me with a dream to start a successful business, I guide them through three success keys: Key #1 – Planning, Key #2 – Taking the Right Actions, and Key #3 - Assessing/Reflecting.

Key #1 - Planning

Good financial plans include all the facets of your life — both personal and professional. Every plan starts with a destination in mind — what do you see when you think of your ideal future? Knowing how to get from A to Z begins with knowing what Z looks and feels like. To bring that dream into focus, I help my clients work with their plans to quantify them into measurable, achievable metrics. These metrics then become the decision-making tools you need to map out the steps that will move you to your destination.

Planning for Results

For example, one client wanted to start her own salon. Her end goal as a business owner was to not only replace her current income from her job but triple it — a total of $120k of pre-tax income. This is when financial mentorship becomes important. I helped her with some projections based on her research and my knowledge to nail down both the start-up costs and the initial operating cash. By reverse-engineering the monthly cash needs of her dream salon, we were able to work out what total cash and financing she would need to support her business and personal needs through those tough six months of start-up. By creating a projected income statement, we then determined how many clients she would need to earn her dream income from the salon. On paper, this plan was a great beginning for her.

My partner Ida had this to add about her recommendations for start-ups. "Regardless of its size, it's critical to properly set up the business right at the beginning. Get your business number from the government and learn the basic tax steps that relate to you. Will you pay wages or dividends? What about source deductions? Keep in mind that hiring a good accountant is a good investment. That's where you'll get profitable advice.

"Also essential to your plan is an excellent tax strategy," continued Ida. "It's important to stay current, especially with the tax department. What many business owners don't realize is that late filing penalties and interest are not tax deductible, so you essentially pay tax twice on that money. Not filing isn't good, either.

"A client who hadn't filed taxes for years was a sole proprietor and a single mom. She was scared she owed the government a bunch of money. Once we cleaned up her files, we discovered the government owed her $30,000 in child tax benefits she had never claimed. A great relationship with a designated accountant and on-time filing of your taxes is the best way to stay in the CRA's good books. Why waste energy dodging the tax man when you could be spending that energy growing your business?"

Planning Actionable Steps

There's such excitement as budding business owners create the big picture of their dream companies. But there's a second stage to planning that's equally important. Once the excitement of your vision fades and reality sets in, you need to realize that the idea of Big Goals can be exhausting. Without planning the small steps you need to take towards the goal, all motivation can be lost.

When you have no clients, finding 2,000 clients seems impossible! A half marathon feels like a death wish when you're exhausted from your first walk! Whether you are starting a business or beginning a journey of personal change, the end point can often seem more of a deterrent than a motivator. This is where metrics can save you!

Let's go back to our numbers again. A mentor will help you take those seemingly impossible results-based numbers and break them down into manageable action steps. Here's an example. If we assume 2,000 clients gets you to your ideal highest possible income, then 500 would probably get you to your break even income. If you're starting from zero, this is your target for the first year.

You decide to find new clients at networking events and estimate to pick up 5 new clients at every networking event you attend. Working from the best case scenario, to get to 500 clients you would then need to attend 100 networking events (5 per event x 100 events = 500 new clients). Does 100 events still seem like an unimaginable amount?

Let's break it down further. There are 52 weeks in a year, 2 of which you will use for a well-deserved vacation. That leaves 50 weeks to work the business. Attending 100 events in 50 weeks means you must attend 2 events/week to meet your goal. Those2 events/week will get you to your ideal client base in five years. How easy is that!

Having a mentor to guide you through this process is invaluable. Your mentor could be your accountant or a business consultant. I've reaped tremendous benefit from this kind of solid planning both professionally and personally, so I encourage my clients to get into the habit of putting all their goals into quantifiable, concrete terms. I want them to experience every benefit possible!

Key #2 – Taking the Right Actions

So let me ask you a question: "Have you ever been in a place in your life where you've thrown the proverbial spaghetti against the wall hoping and praying that something would stick? As we start something new, our first actions can often be like this. While without action, none of your dreams will turn into reality, it's important not to just continue throwing spaghetti!

Wise mentors know that interruptions, experimentation, and course corrections are inevitable as you take those small, consistent steps to reach your goal. To paraphrase a quote by John Lennon, "life happens to you when you're making other plans."

I remember my first conversation with a client who is a mortgage professional. She was "burning the candle at both ends" because of work and family obligations. She was torn between her desire to reach her business goals and her need to spend quality time with her children. At the end of each day, she was exhausted and discouraged.

She knew her ultimate income goal, her margins, and the number of clients she needed. What she didn't know was how much work it would take to gain an additional client. Moreover, she had no idea exactly how many hours she was currently working. How could she possibly determine how many hours were enough?

More Numbers! We decided that one of her action steps was to track her time and activities and determine how many of each type of event and each type of meeting would generate a new a client. Once we knew that, we scheduled those activities regularly, plus we eliminated all the busy work she was doing that she discovered wasn't contributing to her success.

With her action plan in hand, she then knew that her week was over as soon as she had processed all the deals on her desk and made five new contacts. Her final step was to congratulate herself for achieving those weekly benchmarks.

Key #3 – Assessing/Reflecting

Let's go back to our spaghetti example. It's important to look at what sticks, question why it stuck, and then duplicate or replicate what worked. Measuring results that are tied to actions is so, so important. By now you've probably clued into how much I love numbers!

If I want to build a business that I know will take five years, then I need to evaluate each month and each year to make sure of the following:

- Are the assumptions I made when quantifying my original goal still valid?
    - o Are economic conditions the same?
    - o Were there unforeseen personal events that got in the way?
    - o Were my costs estimations too high or margin estimates too low? Was my time commitment over-zealous?

- If my assumptions are current and my results were different, what caused the difference?
    - o Did I underestimate the need for my product or service?
    - o Did I achieve substantially more with marketing than I anticipated?

- o Did I underestimate the time required to run the business, which decreased my ability to do the actions that my metrics required of me?

As part of this reflection process, I remind my clients that all initial projections — those "make-believe" figures — can never be based on a reality that doesn't exist yet. Over time, real numbers show what is and isn't possible. That is why goals are meant to be flexible, not carved in stone.

Refuse to be harsh with yourself if you find you've fallen short of your expectations. Learn from your mistakes and misconceptions, and pat yourself on the back for every success — large or small. Then set new goals based on the information that's been revealed in your assessment.

At Colby•Steckly, we take our own advice. I generate monthly progress reports about our business. During our quieter times, Ida and I take time to celebrate what we've accomplished. When a new year approaches, we start dreaming about and planning for the next important goals.

Just recently I watched Ida do a little happy dance because she got a new client! When you work for yourself, you are the only boss who can provide well-deserved praise and recognition. That acknowledgement of success is a heady motivator!

Choose Your Mentors Wisely

Regardless of which key you're using — planning, acting, or reflecting — a great mentor can assist you with each stage of your business. For example, your strength may not be sales and marketing, so you may need a sales mentor who will transform those business goals into a workable, step-by -step marketing plan, complete with quantifiable results.

You may need a financial mentor to help assess your personal budget to determine cash flow requirements for your business. You may need a personal mentor to help you reflect and course correct or to congratulate you on your success. Start-ups and successful entrepreneurs alike need outside perspectives and support to help take their businesses to new heights.

Your action step: find a mentor to help you use these keys or mentor you regarding your personal or business goals. You'll be glad you did!

Reflections

1.
When I visualize my ideal business goals, what is the picture I see?

2.
What kind of financial plan do I have in place, or do I need help to create one?

3.
Who are the mentors I can count on for business advice?

4.
Am I working harder than I need to — is it time to review my plan?

MENTORING
WOMEN LEADERS

Joanne Kirk

Joanne Kirk is a Consultant with Investors Group Financial Services Inc.

Raised on a farm, Joanne has experienced entrepreneurship from an early age and her background taught her the values of ethics, honesty, and taking pride in her work.

In the last 30 years, Joanne has been in careers that focused on relationship building roles. She has held various management roles, run her own small business, and has trained and mentored people. She understands the importance of treating people like she would want to be treated. Joanne's life experience enables clients to relate to her and gives them the confidence that they are understood and appreciated. She is passionate about building long term relationships and is energized when clients achieve their long and short term goals.

Her personal legacy is to give back to the community through charitable giving and helping donors and charities find better ways to give for today and for the future. Joanne holds the designation of Fellow Chartered Insurance Professional (FCIP) and Elder Planning Counsellor (EPC). She is a graduate of the University of Calgary, Faculty of Continuing Education-Business Management.

In her spare time, she loves golfing, curling, music, making wine, and she enjoys spending time entertaining family and friends.

The Entrepreneurial Dream

Joanne Kirk

Is running your own business for you? I believe everyone, at some point in their lives, has asked themselves this question.

I come from generations of entrepreneurs. My grandparents immigrated to Canada in the late 1880's, settled in southeastern Saskatchewan and became farmers. They worked hard raising cattle and growing grain. They were self-sufficient, provided a helping hand to neighbours and supported their community. Despite the many challenges and obstacles, they built homes, schools, and churches without the luxuries we take for granted today.

Was I destined to be an entrepreneur as my parents and grandparents were? Perhaps. The answer wasn't always so clear. I have been both an employee and self-employed, and have an appreciation for both. It has been a journey of self-discovery leading me to what I do today and, while some of the discoveries were surprising, it has provided me with an "attitude of gratitude."

I am grateful to have the opportunity to work with people and companies, collaborating on strategies for all stages of their life, creating, building, and protecting wealth for their personal and business financial success. I also help implement charitable giving strategies for donors and non-profit organizations, building consistent cash flow for charities, and creating longevity for those who want to leave a legacy for the future.

In any life there are elements of risk. However, when you start your own business, you increase your exposure to serious financial risk. If it's what you really want, if your family fully supports your dream, and if you're willing to put in the hours of hard work, then becoming an entrepreneur can be extremely rewarding.

Your Initial Steps

Visit government service centers and local business organizations. Research the sort of business you want to start and take off your rose-colored glasses. Is there a market? Is a franchise more to your liking? If yes, are there any available in your area?

You'll have to test your idea through development of a solid business plan, which will identify key business planning areas. Check on government funding or assistance from your city, province, or the federal government. Your business idea may fit a category of business that government is actively encouraging through tax breaks, subsidies, or interest-free loans.

If your initial research tells you your dream is feasible, confer with a business lawyer and an accountant. Utilizing a financial planner is an efficient way to understand and organize options, spot potential pitfalls, and develop initial thoughts.

Protect Yourself Against Claims by Creditors

Along with business ownership, comes increased exposure to liability. Whenever possible, avoid providing personal guarantees for business debt. If you're un-incorporated or incorporated and required to give personal guarantees on behalf of the company, you may want family assets in your spouse's name to help insulate your family from possible creditor claims. But you'll need to do this either before you start the business or when the business is solvent.

If your business is incorporated and has built up surplus cash, consider moving it to a holding company to help reduce exposure to future creditors. These are just a couple "creditor proofing" strategies to be considered.

Sole Proprietorship?

The simplest small business structure is a sole proprietorship. A sole proprietorship is an unincorporated business owned by one person — you. You make decisions, reap profits, and claim all the losses. You are on the hook for all the risks of the business including your personal property and assets.

As a sole proprietor, you must …

- Pay personal income tax on all net income generated by your business.
- Make Canada Pension Plan/Québec Pension Plan payments (employer and employee) on your self-employed earnings or pensionable earnings each year.
- Register for the goods and services/harmonized sales tax (GST/HST) and add GST/HST to customer/client billings if your total taxable revenues are more than $30,000.
- Maintain adequate accounting, financial, and other documents to determine tax obligations.
- Have the appropriate life, disability, and critical illness insurance coverage as you no longer are covered by your employer.

The good news …

- You may be able to deduct reasonable expenses incurred to earn business income.
- You can pay reasonable remuneration to family members for work performed.
- You may be able to deduct personal health care/dental plan premiums.

If you foresee start-up losses and have income from other sources, you may prefer a sole proprietorship, which will enable you to deduct business losses on your personal tax return. You may be able to carry forward these losses into future tax years or apply them to a previous tax year depending on your situation.

Incorporation: now, later or never?
If you're like most unincorporated small business owners, you're likely contemplating these thorny questions: Should I incorporate? If so, when's the best time? If not, why not? Incorporation raises a diverse array of issues: length of time you've been in business, your personal cash-flow needs, relative profitability of your business, and provincial personal and corporate tax rates.

If you need all of the profits from your business to support your personal cash-flow needs, incorporation may not be for you. The cost of setting up and maintaining the corporation could outweigh the tax benefits. But when your financial position allows you to retain some of your business profits inside the company, incorporation could deliver significant tax advantages.

When it comes to taxes, incorporation can be a double-edged sword. If you're in the initial stages of your business, it's usually advisable not to incorporate because losses incurred by an incorporated business can't flow through to shareholders. In those early stages, you're better off being able to use those losses personally against other income.

Get a Written Financial Plan
"A goal without a plan is a dream." Author, Elbert Hubbard

Financial Planning is a general term used by most professional advisors — but not all financial plans are created equal. Your financial plan should be a perfect fit for your life as it is today, easily and quickly adaptable to the constant changes and focused on achieving your longer term personal and business goals.

The value of obtaining financial advice is that it brings clarity to your dreams. In fact, an Ispos Reid analysis in 2010 states that Canadians at any age and income level can benefit from having a financial advisor.*

Planning Retirement

Your retirement may be just around the corner or years away. Regardless of when you plan to wind down the business, it's never too early to plan for sufficient income once you move to a new chapter in your life.

Avoid the danger of relying exclusively on the sale proceeds from your business. For some business owners, it may be advantageous to contribute to a Registered Retirement Savings Plan (RRSP), Tax Free Savings Account (TFSA), or corporate investing. Consider tax advantaged mutual funds and permanent life insurance for non-registered investments, as growth in these investment vehicles may be tax-sheltered until you redeem them.

There are also many reasons to set up a holding company. It can offer limited liability to trade creditors and even when the active business ceases, the corporation can still preserve tax deferral, providing a larger pool of capital to fund retirement.

Taxes

The fact of the matter is a successful business will pay taxes. Fortunately, you can take steps to reduce the taxes you pay today and minimize taxes on your estate.

Tax efficiency can be achieved by income-splitting. It can be accomplished through partnership with a family member, with a salary to a family member, or have a family member own shares in the business. This means the family member receiving the salary must provide some service to the business and that salary must be reasonable in light of the services provided. Look into this opportunity as you begin to set up the business and assess the merits of the idea for your circumstances. You can have the structure put in place in advance even if it's not desirable at the time, and utilize it later.

It's never too early to plan your business exit strategy. If you're planning on selling all or part of your business at some point, confirm with your accountant whether you're eligible for the lifetime capital gain exemption and what steps need to be taken.

Unfortunately, we can't eliminate taxes. However, we can use wise business practices to minimize or defer income taxes that would otherwise be payable. Have a complete tax review to identify all the tax planning strategies available to you. After all, the tactics you employ today will help you reap rewards at tax time next year.

Business Continuation

What would happen to your business if you were taken away from it, even temporarily? If you're like most small business owners, the odds are your years of careful nurturing and building could tumble down without your energetic hands on the reins — because you are your business.

A buy-sell provision is probably the most important component of any business protection plan. The agreement spells out the terms and conditions of your departure and allows successors to assume control of the business efficiently in the event of your death, disability or retirement. A fully funded buy-sell agreement can ensure that a key individual, or their family, is looked after in any of those circumstances.

As a business owner, you understand the need to protect against risks to your capital assets. That's why you have fire, theft, and other forms of insurance. An often overlooked risk faced by nearly every business is the temporary loss of vital human capital — a business owner — due to a disability as the result of an accident or an extended illness, perhaps even a life-threatening critical illness.

Consider the following:

- 90% of Canadians have at least one risk factor for heart disease or stroke.* *
- The disability rate increases steadily with age beginning around age 25 — adults aged 45 to 54 have a disability rate of 15.1 per cent.***
- On average, 500 Canadians will be diagnosed with cancer every day.****

You spent a lot of time developing and implementing your business plan. It continues to evolve as your business grows and prospers. Your business continuation plan demands the same attention to detail. Enlist a professional to be sure your goals and needs are matched to the right insurance products for your situation.

You Can't Take It With You

After many years of building your business, you want to ensure the people you care most about inherit your legacy in an orderly fashion. A solid estate plan can eliminate conflict among your heirs and ensure your estate goes to whom it was intended without delay. Your will is the centerpiece of your estate plan along with Power of Attorney and a Health Care Directive.

As you think about dividing assets, account for tax that will ultimately erode your estate. If an equal distribution of assets is important and you are not careful, a failure to account for capital gains tax could result in an unequal allocation.

In conclusion:

It takes a tremendous amount of effort, confidence, drive, and perseverance to get a business from its infancy stage and into operation. Hurdles and obstacles are commonplace and it is only a matter of "when" they are going to arise and not "if" they are going to happen.

Business owners are faced with financial challenges deserving special attention and care. There is a high volume of information available for business and personal financial issues. Advice has never been more important. Information is not knowledge; neither is it wisdom. Knowledge is built upon information and wisdom is to know what to do with that knowledge.

Build your team of experts to help you navigate the maze of business ownership. A well thought out plan for your financial future is an integral part of the building the life you want for yourself, your family, and your business. The reward can outweigh the risks long term if the risks are managed well.

*Source: Ipsos Reid Canadian Financial Monitor special analysis for IFIC. 2010.

** Risks include smoking, alcohol, physical inactivity, obesity, high blood pressure, high blood cholesterol, diabetes. Tracking Heart Disease and Stroke. Heart and Stroke Foundation. Released June 2009.

*** Statistics Canada, Participation and Activity Limitation Survey, 2006.

**** General cancer statistics at a glance, Canadian Cancer Society, May 8, 2012.

Reflections

If you can answer "yes" to these questions, you may have what it takes to run your own business.

1.
Do you like making your own decisions?

2.
Do you have an incredible work ethic?

3.
Do you relish competition?

4.
Are you passionate about your idea?

5.
Do you adapt to change easily and work well with others?

6.
Can you recover after challenges and obstacles are thrown at you?

7.
Do you have the physical and emotional strength to work long hours, up to seven days a week?

8.
Do you clearly know your personal strengths and weaknesses?

9.
Can your lifestyle withstand a lower income while your business gets underway?

10.
Do you plan ahead, meet deadlines, and routinely exercise high levels of self-discipline?

11.
Are you and your family prepared for the hard work and the lifestyle change?

MENTORING
WOMEN LEADERS

Shauna Madsen

Shauna Madsen has been sticking her nose in other people's business for 27 years as a business development specialist. She has been a nominee for Business of the Year with the Chamber of Commerce, awarded Chistopher Leader by her peers, and won an award in 2001 for her own business plan.

The shelf in her office is home to five awards, platinum and gold from Marcom International, recognized for creative excellence with her publication design for Womanition Magazine from 2009 to 2014.

She brings to the table an intuitive creativity to business plan development and she has worked with hundreds of entreprenuers, coaching and mentoring them through the business planning process and helping to launch their companies.

Building the Foundation Before the Walls Go Up

Shauna L.B. Madsen

It was 1988 when Amika Stationery Services came into being. Starting a business seemed like an easy undertaking at the time. After all, I had the support of my grandfather, a commercial printer with a reputation in the industry as the best typesetter and proof-reader the industry has ever had in the city. He was a master craftsman and he sealed business deals on a handshake among his network of industry chums. I spent a lot of time with him, watching, asking a million questions and learning to absorb only as much knowledge as he felt I needed. Though he was happy to share, he came from a world where women didn't belong in the industry; it was a man's trade.

Grandpa was a trade printer, providing services to commercial printing houses across the province. I would stand clear of the heat radiating from the pot of lead he melted over a propane enduced flame. He cast his own lead type, creating individual characters in various point sizes from his antique linotype machines. He would lay the type by hand, one character at a time, setting each letter upside and backward to create full tabloid pages of text — perfectly aligned and proofread as he blocked the paragraphs to make the pages ready for the press. He was a master.

His passion for the written word, for accuracy and style, was infectious. I bought a manual foil printing press with rolls upon rolls of multi-coloured foil. At that time, the foil press was as manual a process as the work my grandfather did on a page, yet on a much smaller scale. He created beautiful tabloid size pages, whereas I could cover nothing larger than an envelope.

I had a few friends and relatives who sold jewellery and makeup and they paid me to produce business cards for them on my new foil press. It was a tedious process, with one card at a time placed in the impression area and with a push of a button, I stamped out each shiny business card. It was with high hopes and great ambition that Amika was set to become an empire, one business card at a time.

My mother was always supportive of my dreams and ideas and clipped out an ad in the paper for a business program she thought might be of interest to me. A government funded self-employment program was offered to anyone with a business start-up idea, at no cost. I applied and was accepted to begin the program immediately.

My girls were four years and six months old when I started the program. The program hours complimented the childcare schedules at the daycare. It seemed like the perfect solution — I would be able to run my business at home with the freedom to schedule my time around the needs of the girls. For a single mother, the prospects of getting a job that paid enough to support the three of us and offer the same flexibility was slim and did not appeal to me in the least. I wanted to explore my own horizons — with my foil press.

Fifteen people ranging in ages from 30 years old to 65 years young made up an eclectic mix of business ideas in the 10-week training program. Each week of interactive learning finished with a completed section of our business plans and one step closer to launching our companies.

The first week began with self-exploration exercises: who am I, what makes me happy, personal drivers, and time management. The facilitator covered topics such as personal budgeting with "what if" scenarios that offered a wake up call to those who were accustomed to earning a regular pay cheque every two weeks.

My business idea was simple. I was going to print business cards for every Fifth Avenue Jewellery person in Edmonton on my foil press and in my basement. My father came for a visit and, with his incredible skill as a machinist, he automated my foil press, giving me 300 imprints an hour instead of 40.

As we continued with the ten segments of writing our business plans, my struggle began when we took to the streets to determine whether there was a market for our product or service. I quickly learned that there weren't enough Fifth Avenue Jewellery sales people in all of Canada to reach the revenue I wanted, not to mention, I would need a team of people just like me, along with several foil presses to produce the volumes to earn the income I had dreamt about. I was at a crossroad with a decision to make, either change my direction and product or get a job.

The instructor explained the secret to success at start-up is to find a need in the market that no one else is satisfying. He encouraged me to go back to my market research and start again, which I did. While researching the outskirts of the printing industry, I went to the paper companies to see what they were doing and what was new or upcoming for paper products. The sales rep showed me samples of two new papers made from recycled material. He explained that this was going to be the new kid on the block; no one was selling it yet. Bellbrook and Passport were the lines of paper; they were expensive and not very attractive.

I took samples back with me to try on my foil press, with little success. The fibres in the paper interfered with the heat of the press and the foil didn't take. I wasn't giving up, my intuition played a huge part as I continued my investigation to learn what printers were doing and the products they were offering. I met a couple of commercial printers who offered me a trade rate for printing if I could find customers who were interested in buying stationery printed on recycled paper.

I set out to learn all about the paper recycling process and how many trees were saved with every order of letterhead, business cards or envelopes. I learned how the papers were made and discovered the negative impact the bleaching process had on our environment. It was my goal to become the expert on recycled paper.

I immediately revised my business concept, went into class and presented my new business direction to my fellow students. Amika Stationery Services became the first company in Edmonton to offer recycled paper products to businesses and "green" organizations. I completed my business plan and set out for a bank loan to fund my start up, mainly to help purchase my $15,000 computer.

The program I took opened doors, provided me with the tools I needed to create a business with a greater chance of succeeding, all because I had a plan. Over the course of many years I rewrote my plan on a yearly basis and it became my road map.

The advantage I have always had in my business is my appreciation for quality market research. Understanding the market, the potential risks, and what my competition is doing, has helped to identify market trends, consumer behaviour, and ultimately, learn the needs of my customers.

Amika was named after my two girls, Amy and Erika, and it grew up alongside my girls to become Madsen Studios. With my background in art and my new passion for technology, graphic design eventually became the core of what we offered. Under the same name in 2005, I opened an art gallery/flower boutique and continued to provide design support. For the artists who showcased their work at my gallery, I provided business-planning and marketing support.

Continuous learning to compliment the changing needs of my customers and the growth of my business included multiple marketing courses and a refresher business program in 2001 where I realized my zeal for business plan development. Complimenting my design service with marketing consultation and business plan development expanded the company and thanks to my daughter Erika, who created the name, we rebranded as Madsen Avenue.

CYBF (Canadian Youth Business Foundation) approached me in 2005 and asked that I join them to review business plans and sit on the loan review committee. When I sold my gallery in 2009, I took a contract to teach a government funded self-employment training program, a full circle opportunity for me. I began my entrepreneurial journey with a similar program and was eager to facilitate and share 20 years of ups and downs with new entrepreneurs, guide them through the process of writing their business plans, and help to launch their start ups.

Business planning has become almost second nature to me and having reviewed, written or assisted with over 650 business plans, I am still excited by the possibilities.

I drop in on a former student now and again to order a pizza and check up on how he is doing with his three-year-old venture. His business is growing and he attributes his success to the business planning process we worked through together.

It has been my experience during my time as a facilitator that a very small percentage of new businesses ever open their doors. For some, it is a lack of capital, for others, the idea or the passion behind the idea lacks the strength or endurance needed to get through the initial stage. Factors can also stem from unrealistic expectations.

The planning process adds an objective perspective to the business when emotions blind an enthusiastic entrepreneur. Believing in an idea is essential to be successful, however, belief alone is not enough. Market research, a competition analysis, and well developed financial forecasts help to paint a picture of possibilities or threats and prepare the business for the "what ifs".

One student I worked with was a nurse who wanted her own practice, had the seed money for start up and her plan was well developed. When it came time to write her financial plan, we worked on her cash flow projections together. After nine sections of the plan were written, it wasn't until we reviewed the financials to realize it wasn't possible to generate enough revenue to meet her expenses; she proved the merits of a plan and the advantage of putting it to paper first. Working through the planning process saved her from signing a five year lease on commercial space.

In a couple of situations when I have developed feasibility plans for clients, the research determined their buisness ideas were not viable. One client chose to ignore my findngs and invested more than one million dollars in the start up. Her doors were closed within nine months.

Plans are intentions, goals and aspirations put to paper, backed with sound research that proves the business idea is viable. We may not be able to predict how the business will unfold over a three-year period, but we can negate some of the risk and uncover or discover opportunities that exist in the shadows of the competition.

People tend to spend more time planning their holidays than they do their businesses. Seasoned entrepreneurs understand that working on the business is as important as working in the business. When I think back to my very first week of the program in 1988, when we discussed the importance of time management, "working on the business" was scheduled into our calendars. Planning creates a proactive mindset, strengthens our ability to solve problems, and lays the foundation for growth.

Reflections

1.
Is owning and running your own business in your future? Do you know what it will take to make it happen? Are you emotionally invested in your business idea?

2.
If you do own your business, do you have a working plan?

3.
Who is your customer, where are they, and what do they want? Are you filling a need in the market?

4.
Do you step back and take the time to work on your business?

5.
Do you know who your competition is and what sets you apart from them?

6.
A business plan is a series of well thought out and researched intentions — where do you intend to be in three to five years?

Testimonials

I recently had the pleasure of having Shauna facilitate a self-employment program I was enrolled in. She offered a wealth of information with real-world experience. Her energy and enthusiasm was infectious and a real asset to the program; I can see why she has been successful in all her business endeavours. I look forward to seeing her succeed again. *Lino Iacobellis, Checkpoint Manager at Edmonton International Airport*

One of the great attributes Shauna has as a Communication Specialist is her ability to listen. This comes about because she has a sincere desire to understand. Thanks Shauna! Hope to work with you again! *Bonnie Hoffmann, Life Celebrant, Speaker, Cemetery Advocate*

I was one of many artists well represented by Shauna while she had Madsen studios in the Highlands district of Edmonton. The gallery was unique, fabulous and vibrant. During those years she envisioned and implemented a Highlands annual art show and brought such enthusiasm, imagination and marketing plans to it that it became the summer event of the neighborhood. She spearheaded this by leadership and encouraging teamwork with the other local businesses. Her gifts of strategic planning, creativity, great communication skills and zest for life leave me firmly convinced she can succeed in anything she could desire. Also, that she can assist others in their climb to the stars....Shauna rocks. *Patricia Doyle, Owner, Bella Vista Glass Art ~ Glass and metal artisan and teacher*

Shauna and I have worked together for years! The reason being is she GETs me. She got all my crazy ideas about colour, layout, and design on how I wanted the outcome of my magazine to look and hence from our peers we've won platinum and gold awards. I told her many times I thought she was a genius. The truth is she is one of the most creative, genuine, caring, and thoughtful persons I have met. Shauna has really become family to me as I call her my "sister". I love our conversations and am extremely happy when the phone rings and it's her. I can always count on Shauna Madsen to deliver her promises whether it's personal or business. Everyone who knows Shauna pays high regard to her brilliant talent in marketing and thought processes. Womanition misses her! *Dorothy Briggs, Womanition Magazine*

Shauna Madsen
780.803.4250
madsens@shaw.ca

MENTORING
WOMEN LEADERS

Wendy Olson-Brodeur

Money is a formidable force in our first world lives, an energy that affects the very essence of our well-being.

Certified Financial Planner, and owner of "The Financial Divorce Specialist Inc", Wendy Olson-Brodeur is on a mission to share her knowledge and compassion, helping you navigate your money issues as you journey through the realities of life.

One of the few in Canada to claim the Chartered Financial Divorce Specialist designation, this enlightened professional's passion is to EDUCATE clients so they can make wise wealth decisions, ENRICH their experience with a more holistic understanding of their money "personality", and to EMPOWER them to take greater control of their financial situation now, to be thus better prepared in the future.

Wendy's company name "Wealth Wellness Inc" succinctly says it all.

Once Upon A Penny – The Many Money Lessons of Life

Wendy Olson-Brodeur

Life is full of lessons. If only I would have listened when I was younger…

But then I wouldn't have had the wealth of experiences that make me who I am today, a Certified Financial Planner and Chartered Financial Divorce Specialist, educated on all aspects of money, who, after more than a quarter century in banking, decided there was more to preparing people for life's contingencies than selling RRSPs.

At that point, I had seen so much of life's tragedies, disappointments, and reversals, and I'd taken away the lessons. I learned from my own experience of being trapped in an abusive relationship, compelled to stay due to lack of financial resources. I learned from my years working in the professional banking world where it's still a challenge for women to be seen as "promotion worthy" as their male counterparts. I learned from watching my family confront my father's unexpected illness at a early age.

I saw how the aspect of money was woven into each and every scenario, positively or negatively. To truly be of any real financial help to my clients, I knew I had to take more of a holistic approach. How does money affect your world, your stress levels, your ability to react to the challenges of life? I knew I could guide my people in discovering the right answers specific to their own situations.

Knowledge is power...ful! With knowledge, you're in control, empowered to make those life-changing decisions from an educated standpoint. From my passion to **educate, enrich, and empower** the people I serve, my company "Wealth Wellness Inc" was born.

Just as life is a flow of energy, I believe that money, too, can flow freely, even overflow, or conversely, get dammed up, even dry up. When I talk money with clients, I focus first on cash flow. It's not just where the money is coming from, but where is it going? Interesting that our education system prepares us to land the job, to start the business, but neglects to teach us how to manage that first pay cheque. Where do we learn about financial planning, emergency funds, protecting our money, or even the most basic financial life skills like balancing a budget, applying for a mortgage, using credit cards? Money is a formidable force in our society. The idea of living without it is terrifying. Base human emotions, like greed and revenge, can turn money into a veritable weapon. How to have power over your money without it having power over you?

In his Millionaire Mind seminars, Harv Eker describes our "money personalities", a concept that really helped me understand the "why" behind my clients' varied money behaviours. According to Eker, there are four distinct money types. "Savers" are analytical, even anal in their detailed tracking of every penny. Obviously, they tend to understand their financial situation in exact detail, which can be a positive, yes, but they can be seen as miserly, unwilling to let go and spend money on anything.

The "spenders", their polar opposites, revel in lavishing money, living utterly in the moment, and in overdraft, with little regard to the negative consequences of over spending. In fact, their unfettered generosity and penchant for shopping can become a huge problem. Avid credit users, left unrestrained, they're major candidates for bankruptcy.

"Avoiders" usually operate from fear, an aversion to anything financial in life. They think if they just don't look too closely at that fine print on the statement that describes the interest calculation, then they're protected from any consequences. This "ignorance is bliss" approach can only last for so long before harsh reality bursts their pretty "budget".

The forth type Eker coined "Monk", as they often lead a simple life, trusting that the universe will look after them. Deep believers in the karmic "what goes around comes around" theory, they're not likely to do any financial planning.

There is no right or wrong type; more just a result of your upbringing, learned beliefs, present situation, and more. If you can identify with your type's behaviour, then dealing with strategies around money is easier. Understanding the motivation behind your actions, you can learn from past mistakes when creating your financial plan for the future.

The reality is we never know what's around the corner; it could be illness, divorce, or disability, even sudden death. Holistic financial planning helps you achieve the necessary balance. Save some, spend some, identify your needs, choose your long-term goals. Your money "map" should be carefully charted, judiciously followed, and yet, we do more pre-planning in our selection of just the right outfit for that special occasion, than we do for our financial future.

All I know today is a result of lessons learned from my past — from the hopelessness of my abusive relationship that, penniless, I was unable to escape, to watching my father fall ill in his mid fifties and pass away ten years later, the health expenses having decimated the entirety of his retirement savings, to seeing my mother struggle to support my brother who's unable to work due to a debilitating condition. The lessons here are evident about money and balance — certainly live in the present, but definitely plan for the future!

Make the time to ponder future possibilities, probabilities, the "what ifs", the great experiences you'd like to have, and the legacy you'd like to leave. Protect your family and your assets. Start your own emergency fund. Make a plan NOW! You'll never regret it.

In my financial planning seminars, the majority of my audience will typically answer that their house is their greatest asset. Personally, I like to think it's our ability to earn an income. When something thwarts our earning potential, it's devastating to immediate cash flow, a must have to finance our preferred life style. When you're faced with a crisis that de-rails your income, it's even more pressure added to your already stressful financial situation. So why do we tend to wait till we hit that wall?

Becoming money conscious is simply making time to take an honest look at the fundamentals of your spending habits. Most of us just hate budgets, the mere word sending shivers though our bodies. I encourage my clients to tackle the task one step at a time. Get out those pay stubs, bank and credit card statements. Establish your basic living expenses, food, housing, tax, transportation, and utilities. Set priorities. Yes, you need to eat, but always in a restaurant?

Calculate any major spending associated with desired GOALS, debt reduction, home renovations, vacations, eventual retirement — know your number. Track all the spending you do on "WANTS"; that new pair of black shoes to join the other dozen now boring pairs in your closet.

We're creatures of habit. Stuck in our comfort zone, we really don't want to change. Along comes the life crisis forcing us to do it anyway. The difference being with a little pre-planning, we would have been prepared! Life is about choices. Make the right financial ones.

I suggest you take control now before an unforeseen event renders you out of control. Look at your spending categories, set those priorities, and start to make the choices and the changes, before they're foisted upon you. If you've not started retirement saving, determine how much you'll need. If insurance is a wise choice for your healthy spouse, then look at costs. I am here to help you get on track with all this, and keep you there. You need a professional's help! If not me, find one with whom you resonate.

Managing credit is another challenge for the financially savvy wannabe. I got my first credit card in high school. So much fun...spending money I didn't have. Yeehaw! The statement would come, I'd say to myself, "Oh, I won't pay this month. I need the cash. I'll just double the payment next month!" That approach is very effective... if you want to ruin your credit rating! I suggest my clients determine their monthly spending allotment and pay that money on the card in advance. This way you don't exceed your budget, but you do establish yourself as a good credit risk, and can still qualify for all the proffered perks.

In North America, we can obtain insurance coverage not just for the eventuality of death, but while we are still alive as well, and much more likely to need the financial help. Do you think my father ever dreamed serious illness would herald an early death right at retirement? Living benefits could help in the event of a short-term injury, long-term disability, or terminal illness. Even with health history, you may still be eligible. It's worth your time to investigate with an experienced, qualified professional whether you may actually need multiple insurance strategies.

It's been said that people who have the life of their dreams pay themselves first, and spend what's left, while the ones who spend first never have enough for their future. Pay yourself first; even go so far as "dollar-cost averaging", setting up your investment payments as automatic withdrawals.

The fear of losing money is a very real stressor in investing. The easiest solution involves the concept of possibility and probability. If I invest all my resources into one entity, it's both possible and probable that if something happens in that particular industry, the value of that stock will suffer. Conversely, if money is spread out among a number of different companies, industries, even countries, it's still possible they all fail at once, but the probability of that happening is negligible. This technique of "diversification", critical to basic investing, effectively removes the fear of devastating loss.

Book some time in your calendar to write your eulogy. It's one of the most revelatory and empowering exercises you'll ever do. Looking at my life from the perspective of tomorrow being my last day compelled me to head right out and make some major changes. Do you have a WILL? Make the time to get this done, this week!! One of my clients faced extreme tragedy when her husband was suddenly killed, leaving no insurance, no pension, no will. It was tremendously sad. She had to submit extensive paperwork to the provincial trustee just to finance her sons playing hockey. If anyone dares mention the cost of making a will as a deterrent, I don't hold back elaborating in vivid detail the cost of NOT making one!

Drawing up a legal Enduring Power of Attorney and Personal Directive is absolutely essential, as well. Unless an adult assigns someone to oversee his affairs in case of incapacity, the government intercedes. Why would you take that chance?

In my capacity as a CDFS, owner of "The Financial Divorce Specialist Inc", I see a large number of individuals decimated by unforeseen marital dissolution. So many women who married their "Prince Charming", trusting him to faultlessly run all their financial affairs, experience that proverbial rude awakening from the fairy tale, only to find themselves alone and abandoned with no money or property. If you receive an inheritance know that as long as you keep the capital in your own name, it remains yours, but if you divorce any gains must be split.

The bottom line is, no matter how much that Prince loves you, no matter how big his kingdom, it's always best to be financially independent.

We live in such a time of "entitlement". How many times have I seen adult children spending freely, saving nothing, waiting to inherit the "big" money from their parents to dig them out of debt. What if they foil your plans by living a very long time with expensive healthcare needs and actually use up all their savings?

Life is full of lessons. A lot of them revolve around money.

I am Wendy Olson-Brodeur. I can empower you to take control of your money and positively put its power to use, so you can follow Thoreau's wise advice, "Go confidently in the direction of your dreams! Live the life you've imagined."

Happily ever after...

Reflections

Ask yourself…

1.
What lessons have you learned about you and your money?

2.
What is the energy of your money?

3.
What is your money personality? Are you using it to your advantage?

4.
Do you respect money? How is your money flowing? How money conscious are you REALLY?

5.
Do you have your own emergency fund?

6.
What's your plan to stop using debt? Do you use debt in a positive way?

7.
What if you were the next statistic for a disability, illness, or accident? What would you do to pay your bills?

8.
Are you paying yourself first and spending the rest?

9.
If you reference your life to date, what would your eulogy say? You can change your legacy now. The choice is yours!

10.
Don't you think you need an experienced financial professional to help you move to the next level?

11.
Why are you putting it off yet another day?

MENTORING
WOMEN LEADERS

Grow Your Business

Barb Steckly

Bernadette Geronazzo

Cheryl Dyck

Christine Till

Donna McColl

Mary Lou Gutscher

Rita-anne Fuss

Zandra Bell

Barb Steckly

Small in stature, but mighty of heart, when the unstoppable Barbara Steckly sets her mind to achieving an objective, it's a done deal!

Unafraid to put it all on the line to realize her dreams, this ambitious small town farm girl outstripped her modest rural roots, turning a talent for numbers, into the uniquely designed, woman powered, high level bookkeeping empire, "Preferred Client Services", known for its miracle working contributions to clients' overall success.

A strong advocate for mentoring, Barbara has capitalized on the concept to successfully enhance the lives and the livelihood of countless staff members as well.

Out there making a positive difference, Barb Steckly is the brilliant bookkeeper who cares.

Mentorship – The Guide To Greatness

Barb Steckly

We've seen it happen in the movies many times, but in real life, can the underdog actually triumph?

The small town Saskatchewan high school I attended on the 'wrong' side of the river had only six members on our tiny cheerleading squad. The 'good' school, boasting a glowing squad of thirty, was, not surprisingly, the predictable winner of the annual cheerleading championship, year after year after year.

The idea that we would have even the most remote chance of placing first ourselves was laughable, so everyone thought. But we had a dream...and that was about all. I had heard, however, of an innovative American squad performing outstanding acrobatic routines requiring very advanced levels of fitness and coordination. Undaunted, I tracked them down and, with single-minded perseverance, eventually convinced them to help. I had, in essence, unwittingly just set up my first mentor/protégée collaboration!

Advising us to practice in secret, our savvy mentors helped us create amazing routines. We even persuaded our track team to include us in their grueling workouts to ensure we had the enhanced fitness levels to perform the new techniques. Our "little squad that could" toiled all summer vacation to perfect the choreographed moves we hoped would take us to the top.

When the big day came, very nervous, but extremely well prepared, we took our dream to the stage in our homemade uniforms. Despite their tentative smattering of polite applause, we gave that audience our all. The performance was flawless! Even the judges had never seen leading edge cheerleading like ours, never mind the rest of the stunned crowd. As the last notes of our final music died away, there was a moment of dead silence...followed by the deafening applause of a standing ovation as the judges posted scores showing we had won! Yes, just like out of the movies, we had humbled the mighty and it was sublime!

Without our mighty mentors, though, we wouldn't have had the practical knowledge of the routines, the street smarts to conceal our progress, nor the emotional support of leaders who'd already had that vital experience of winning and were thus able to inspire us to summon up the strength, stamina, and courage to succeed. Most importantly, we would not have had anyone who believed in us, our power to win.

Now tell me mentoring is not essential in creating women leaders!

After graduation, my very first job was a customer service position with a finance company, not very well paying and even less challenging. But I had ambitions. After all, I was a champion cheerleader! I informed Human Resources my intention was to be branch manager. They laughed. A woman in a management role?!! Well, she'd never be taken seriously! Useless at the hardcore money collection calls, especially a girl as young and petite as that!

Once again, I was fortunate to find a strong mentor in my regional supervisor who knew a determined woman when he saw one. He didn't discourage my initiative, but he was bluntly honest as to the extreme degree of difficulty I was facing if I really wanted to achieve such an unlikely promotion. The best thing he did for me, however, was provide me with a game plan; clear and specific steps I could take to bring me closer to my goal.

Following his astute recommendations, I enrolled in all the available courses, absorbed all the practices, policies, and procedures, even became the official IT expert, converting most of our Western Canadian offices to the new computer system. Tiny as I was in stature, I had formidable aspirations, so I developed the skills to tackle those unsavoury hard cases, and learned how to be a tough, competent collector.

For two grueling years I traveled constantly, literally living out of a suitcase. If I wasn't doing the system conversions, to gain supervisory experience, I volunteered for any temporary assignments providing managerial relief. It was challenging, typically thankless, occasionally frightening, but my mentor's encouragement, his confidence in choosing me for the challenging assignments, his unwavering faith in me, that's what gave me the impetus to carry on.

Yes, in the end, I did become the first female branch manager, and the youngest person in that finance company's history to be promoted to that position! Oh, I had ambition, and drive, all right. I had overdrive, but I would never have accomplished my goal had it not been for constructive mentorship.

As a woman starting out in business, or even as a seasoned professional interested in branching out in a new direction, success in your venture is definitely more attainable if you have an established "coach" to count on for that valuable mentoring and support. Just to know that your mentor believes in your talent and potential is a positive morale boost.

My regional supervisor was an excellent example of the mentor model. He definitely listened, and understood my frustrations, but, while he provided invaluable guidance, he was not out there making it easy for me by any means. He had very high expectations of himself, and thus, of me, and although he worked with me to help me focus on my strengths, it was very clear that if I was going to receive that promotion, it would be me, not him, doing the necessary hard work.

Many years later, I had a new dream. I wanted to start my own bookkeeping company; not just any "accounting records reviewing" office, but a notable, professional firm renowned for accomplishing any bookkeeping objective with a high level of excellence. I wanted to create a unique bookkeeping company that would provide additional value to business owners beyond determining the tax man's quarterly share, one that would act as a "partner", offering relevant financial information aligned with entrepreneurs and their goals.

I had a unique vision for staffing, as well. I would provide a workplace where women could use their bookkeeping skills to build solid careers; an environment of excellence where they'd be recognized and well paid for these "value added" contributions I knew we could make to our small business clients' ultimate profitability.

Welcome to Preferred Client Services Group LTD, my dream realized! We work on files from a whole array of industries, giving our bookkeepers the business acumen and "hands on" experience they'd never get working for one company at a time. After several years with us, our highly trained "numbers" experts can handle any bookkeeping assignment with the utmost of professionalism.

Of course, believing passionately in mentoring, I've put the concept to work at my firm to everyone's advantage. Even experienced bookkeepers first joining our company are amazed at how much they need to learn, so certainly mentorship plays a critical role in every new team member's success. Regardless of past experience, each new bookkeeper works alongside a mentor to thoroughly understand our organizational systems and philosophies. Teamwork and collaboration are valued extremely high as the key to innovating the best solutions to our clients' problems.

Does a corporate culture that fosters mentoring produce greater profits? Absolutely! The majority of Fortune 500 companies have ongoing mentorship programs to help alleviate debilitating issues, such as employee retention and low morale. Mentored employees have been found to be happier overall, and are thus more productive. Since productivity increases profitability, mentoring is a proven benefit to the corporate bottom line.

Often the "mentored" grow up within my business to become the mentor, as was the case with one of our bookkeepers who'd previously been unable to find a job situation mentally stimulating enough to satisfy her quick mind. Seeing her true management potential, I had her paired with an appropriate "teacher". Not only did she learn the high-level technical bookkeeping techniques, but developed her supervisory skills, ultimately landing a challenging, dynamic position within our company, perfect for her needs.

Mentoring can be impactful not just when orienting new staff members, but within leadership development programs. Job satisfaction and employee engagement are significantly enhanced when your people are given the opportunity to develop and learn. Mentor/mentee relationships are as varied and unique as the individuals involved. Some, requiring scheduled meetings on a regular basis, are structured with specific action plans and accountability, whereas, in other scenarios, the "protégé" might only feel the need to seek specific guidance from their mentor during a particularly stressful time.

In a formal mentorship program, parameters are clearly designated, and faithfully observed as part of the initial agreement. Commitment is key. There's no point to the process if there's a failure to do the work. Objectives would be discussed and established, but flexibly revisited as the mentee progresses.

Mentoring is not just training. Great mentors give direction sparingly, objectively providing fresh, positive perspectives instead; not telling their protégé what to think, but rather influencing them to use the most empowering thought processes to find the best course of action given their specific situation. In essence, collaborating with your mentor should be a "voyage of discovery". An effective mentor asks probing questions to encourage their charge to dig deep and seek insights to difficult problems by going within, thus developing faith in their instincts.

True mentors inspire their mentees to define their principles, beliefs, and values. As the novice formulates their own personal priorities, outmoded beliefs can be discarded and life decisions seen in a new light.

I'm proud to say so many of my own team members have enthusiastically shared with me that working in my bookkeeping firm has truly transformed and improved their lives, teaching them much, much more than any previous schooling or employment position.

I find recognizing achievements and providing praise for excellence builds the mentee's confidence and inner strength. Conversely the mentor should always teach their charge to view life's failures as learning opportunities. Claiming our right to fail without self-recrimination is one of the keys to successful personal development. When a mentor can reflect back their mentee's own magnificence, help them glory in themselves, imperfections and all, both lives are forever enhanced.

Another type of mentoring, paramount to our company, distinguishes us from the rest. Many of our clients are new "fledgling" businesses, owned by youthful, inexperienced entrepreneurs gifted with all the creative talents in the world, but devoid of financial analysis skills. As their "numbers" experts, we patiently educate these young clients, explaining every detail of their financial reports; showing them how their accounts tell a story that can positively influence their operational decisions and lead them to a much higher level of success.

In essence, money earned has to be substantially more than money spent for a business to be profitable. Seems so simple, yet so many owners, rightfully concentrating on their operations, miss the realities we can untangle from looking at the figures; determining, for example, that the price of a particular product is less than half of its expense to produce. Obviously the product's price needs to be increased or the product itself discontinued, but our entrepreneurs don't know to make this decision until we point these nuances out. Our unique "knowledge transfer mentoring" has resurrected many a sinking venture, through the proficient use of "key performance indicators", control systems and a customized business plan with long term projections. Administering our effective, empathic mentoring, we help that proverbial underdog triumph again and again.

From winning cheerleader, to trailblazing branch manager, to the proud, self-assured president of my very own superlative and innovative bookkeeping domain, there's been one constant in my life that's made me who I am today — the all encompassing power of mentoring. Never be too proud to ask someone "above" you for guidance, in any realm of your life. Galileo says it all very insightfully. "We cannot teach people anything; we can only help them discover it within themselves."

I assure you the potential for greatest is inside you. Let mentoring be its guide.

Reflections

1.
Are there any areas of your business, or even your life in general, you'd like to better understand and/or improve?

2.
Have you thought about seeking out a mentor or even a formal mentorship program to help?

3.
Are you perhaps bogged down by the perception that asking for help is a sign of weakness or inadequacy?

4.
Are you aware that the "needing help means you're weak" concept is an outmoded core belief that has no place in a successful entrepreneur's life?

5.
The way we learn and grow is by seeking guidance from those ahead of us on the path. If you really care about moving ahead, don't you think it's time to get out of your own way?

6.
Don't you think it is also time to seek help in doing just that, get out of your own way?

MENTORING
WOMEN LEADERS

Bernadette Geronazzo

Over the years, Bernadette Geronazzo has empowered organizations that range from the non-profit to publicly traded companies.

Corporate leaders from this wide cross-section of business enterprise have trusted her company at In the Public Eye to provide outside eyes and understanding for their current business challenges. She has helped many to implement creative communication strategies that have enabled them to realize their goals and objectives.

A thoughtful and wise leader, Bernadette has had the privilege of holding Board Member positions, has launched a number of signature events, has been a newspaper columnist, and even a television show host.

As a public relations professional, Bernadette Geronazzo has been recognized by the International Association of Business Communicators with a Gold Quill Award.

Sharing Wisdom

Bernadette Geronazzo

Having been invited here as one of many, I thought you might enjoy reading this letter wherein you may glean some nuggets of wisdom for yourself. It is my intent that you may learn from others, as I have, in order to make your own life a bit easier along the way.

Allow me to begin with one of the most formative decisions that continues to provide me with endless peace and pleasure. My parents modelled the excellence of self-discipline through sports. When I was in the 4th grade, I joined my mother every weekday morning to catch the 5:30 am televised "Yoga with Olga." This was a great TV show. It was here that I learned how to breathe, how to calm my mind, and how to bring strength and confidence into my entire being. Following our yoga practice, I would run to school and train for about 45 minutes in gymnastics before attending my classes. Through these habits of daily exercise, I learned the value of self-discipline. These days, this repetitive early morning endeavor takes the form of hot yoga, a ballet workout, tai chi or a jog outside in the fresh air. I feel centered, strong and focused when I begin my day this way.

Remember **Decisions** are what determine your life. Hopes do not. Wishes do not. Only **Decisions** truly direct where your life will lead. Some of those decisions will be made by others, but the majority will be made entirely of your own volition. Decisions empower the Universe to conspire in ways to manifest your intentions into reality.

One decision that was made externally and had internal shifts for me was the separation and divorce of my parents from when I was between 6 – 10 years of age.

Life Lesson Here? Learn to adapt at an early age!

When you are shipped from one new school to another, over a progression of years; when you find the circumstances are continually new and changing — you learn to be flexible. Along with flexibility another little lesson was learning how far to go in order to be accepted.

It's strange what we will do as young people in order to be accepted, is it not?

My wish is that YOU will choose to be an individual — separate from the crowd, by making choices that are in alignment with your personal beliefs about what is right and just. Following the "crowd" can lead to devastating consequences. As I reflect on it now, I am reminded of the consequences that have befallen those I've watched follow a crowd. When you have time, YOU may want to Google *"Grimm's Brothers +Pied Piper,"* to read an example of what I am referring to.

Be NOT a follower. Be an individual, a unique and different person from the rest, or a leader — if you so desire. Be any of these for your own sake and, most importantly, be **Yourself**.

May you learn to be resourceful, studious, hardworking, and seek to be quick on your feet and in your thoughts. For just as in nature, you will need to figure out whom to befriend, whom to avoid, and whom to stand up against.

In my early years, I learned to pay attention to my surroundings, determine where I wanted to be, and how to stand my ground so I that would not be pushed around.

We grew up on the "tough" side of town. Ours was rather the opposite of the white picket fence with stay-at-home wives, manicured lawns, and luxury cars. Fighting repeatedly for what was right, as a youngster, developed part of my character.

Our father said a few things that became mantras for me. May they strike a resonating chord for own life.

"You MUST set a good example. Younger ones always look up to the older one to see what they are supposed to do."
"Practice so that you can be your best."
"SURE you can do it! You just need to keep at it until the job is DONE."

He was short on praise and always seemed to find areas wherein we could improve. This expectation he had of us — for ongoing excellence — was foundational in helping me set very high standards for myself. In my experience, when you expect nothing but the best from yourself, those around you will often raise their own bar of performance.

My mother was also a lighthouse of wisdom shining through those dark adolescent years.

"Education is FREEDOM," she would say. "When you succeed at school you can succeed in life."

I was lucky because she exemplified style and elegance for me as a girl. Her example helps me — even now — to embrace being a woman. Remember also, "A woman can be over-dressed but never over-elegant" - Coco Chanel.

I hope that by now you KNOW the value of education. Not only through post-secondary education, but as a lifelong pursuit. The world is an ever-changing place. Those who choose to learn new skills and expand their horizons will not only find themselves work, but they also have the opportunity to become valued members in society.

In your own life there will come a time where you need to set very tangible, concrete, and meaningful goals for yourself. If you write them down in the present tense, as if they have already been achieved, they **will** eventually materialize.

Here is an example from my own life: After I had been "kicked out" of the group of girls I used to run with, I found myself quite alone. It gave me the chance to consider what I could do with all this new-found time as I was just entering Junior High. There was a giant, glass case filled with magnificent trophies and awards recognizing all kinds of sports and scholastic achievement. Noticing "Angela Kokot" on many of the name plates, I made a decision.

"My name is going to be on EVERY ONE of those trophies."

I wrote this in my journal that very day. My journal entries grew ever-more concrete as time went on.

I recall writing, "Thank you, I am so happy to be accepting this award for outstanding citizen, top all-around athlete, most congenial student..." I wrote these sentences along with a complete description of how I felt as I was receiving each of those trophies. I constantly visualized myself accepting those awards in the 3 years that followed.

The picture in my mind repeated itself every day as I went to and from classes because I passed that trophy case every day. Consciously, and subconsciously, I knew what my goal was and I dedicated all of my energy to fulfilling that desire.

On the awards night, the gymnasium was decorated with beautiful silver stars edged in silver tinsel hanging at various heights from the ceiling. Students and parents were seated at long tables decorated with white tablecloths and sprinkled with sparkling silver stars. In this dream-like atmosphere I recall feeling joy and delight as I kept hearing my name being called out, again and again, to accept all the awards I had worked to attain.

Have you ever had high expectations only to be devastated by what you encountered in reality?

Such was my experience after I had worked a year to save all my money in order to attend the local university. My illusions of imagined intellectuals and people in sophisticated attire was shattered by the reality that everywhere there were only everyday, ordinary people.

The Learning? "You cannot tell the forest by the trees."

Intellectuals WERE everywhere, I simply had to remove my own prejudiced lenses to see them.

University was where I encountered humility and spectacular failure. I had been so accustomed to success in school that the very notion of failing took me by surprise.

There is a famous saying that goes, "If you want to accelerate your success just double your rate of failure." This means you need to try things that are new and challenging, wherein you may not find immediate success.

At that point in my journey, it meant learning calculus with a tutor, getting extra assistance, and decreasing my course load so that I could focus on fewer courses in order to achieve passing grades.

At about the 2 year mark, I made a number of simultaneous decisions:

- Leave Calgary
- Transfer my education to Montreal
- Leave my job
- Leave my family
- Take out a spontaneous loan
- Venture out completely on my own.

Remember that you only make the best possible decision at the time, given your perspective and the information you have — in that moment. This will alleviate you from berating yourself too much and should absolve you from too much guilt as you look at your own past.

Those decisions I made all those years ago had mixed blessings because my loan was at some outrageous rate of 26%. It took me years to repay! However, my one-way ticket to Montreal where I knew only one student was an amazing learning experience. I was able to work and study while exercising my French and Italian language skills.

Had you been in my position, you too would have: learned how to live within your limited means, sought work that was within your background of skills, and stepped forward when others might have stood still so that you did not get run over.

Living in Montreal taught me to wake up the next morning and deal with the consequences of some poor choices made the night before. It taught me to recognize opportunity and to act quickly as well as decisively. In a big city, "He who hesitates is LOST."

When I eventually returned to Calgary, I will admit that good fortune smiled on me.

I was able to begin a career with The Four Seasons Hotel, complete my education as a Public Relations Practitioner, work in sales, meet the wonderful man who wooed me to become his wife, and I earned my stripes by achieving a Gold Quill from the International Association of Business Communicators. There are many other things I have been blessed to accomplish because I was open to new adventures. I hope you will also have this open perspective for your own life.

At this point, Dear Reader, I would like to impart a few pieces of advice that I know will enhance your life:

1. Buy yourself the best QUALITY you can afford.
   Know that Quality is not necessarily synonymous with a BRAND name.
   Quality in clothing is found in the:
   - Feeling and texture of the fabric
   - Fine and complete stitching
   - Way in which the garment feels on your frame and

- Ability for this garment to provide you with many years of enjoyment as an enduring piece to transcend "fashion."

2. Choose to READ
   In reading you may be able to expand your everyday vocabulary, your ability to express yourself and enhance your ability to be easily understood. I cannot think of a better conduit for personal growth than reading inspiring books, poetry, and newspapers.

3. If you choose to marry someone, REGISTER for what you like in a China pattern
   - There will never again be another occasion where people you know will happily gift you a $500 place setting.
   - Over time you will recognize the enduring value and usefulness of this gift that keeps on giving.
   - Aunts, uncles and grandparents WANT to give you pieces of enduring quality and they can relate to china.
   - IF you fail to register, know that you will be gifted. ceramic cats and many other less-than-desirable items
   - Like me, you may not even like the idea, BUT remember Nike? "Just Do It!". You will be amazed at how much your future self will appreciate this choice as you entertain friends and family in the years to come.

Recommended Reading:

- Desiderata, the poem, by Max Ehrmann
- The Prophet, by Khalil Gibran
- All I Really Need to Know I Learned in Kindergarten, by Robert Fulghum

Reflections

Every woman is like a snowflake: she is comparable to a unique crystalline formation that changes with environmental conditions.

1.
What makes you unique and different?

2.
How can you celebrate this in your life through self-honouring actions and behaviours?

Consider some goals that inspire dreams you want to have come true. It is important to recognize that YOU can only affect YOUR life, so be sure that your goals are for and about YOU exclusively.

1.
Take the time to write out 3 goals you want to achieve in the next 3 months. Remember to articulate the goal in the present-tense, already achieved moment, and be sure you have attached the kinds of positive and energizing emotions to convey how, having achieved this goal now, you feel in your mind and body.

2.
What will you do today to bring you closer to this envisioned future reality?

3.
Record your incremental progress so that you can celebrate your steps along this road to achievement.

Cheryl Dyck

Cheryl Dyck knows business. She has over 28 years of experience in Marketing, Operations, Management, Strategic Planning, Team Development, Security & Forensics, Training, Quality & Process Improvements, Commercial Property Management, Energy Sectors, and Information & Technology.

She knows first-hand what it takes to start and run a successful business and has helped lead businesses from chaos to efficient and profitable enterprises. Customers obtain annual growth between 40% and 300% when Cheryl partners with them to get results.

What she will help you do is assess the current state of your business, identifying the gaps and opportunities. Create the long term plan, to support your personal and business goals and dreams to build a strong empowered results oriented team to support your business goals and help you create a business to strategically exit when you are ready.

Sacrifice, Are YOU holding yourself back?

Cheryl Dyck

As a business owner and a senior executive and business coach, I often get asked about success. How I respond often surprises people. As a coach, there are many key foundational elements that are critical for a business to be successful. I know that business fundamentals mastery is key, along with systems, niche, and team. When we are working on business planning and growth in an organization, the most important key to success starts with the business owner! In the following pages, I will highlight some of the key things that will sabotage your success and how you can take control of your life, your business, and your future.

Let's start by looking at how you adjust to change. Are you fearful and shy away from change for more stability and status quo, or do you jump up and go for it, taking the opportunities that arise without thinking too much about it? Believe it or not, many business owners will shy away from change, for more stability and status quo. The reasons people do this varies from person to person. For me, I embrace change, but support it with a great plan and list of action items to implement. How do you overcome the holdbacks to take advantage of opportunities so you don't sacrifice yourself and your future?

Not Planning just Reacting? — Learn to Plan your future. Stats show that over 50% (I actually think it is higher) of business owners do not have plan for themselves and their business. They react day to day to all the operational things, but never really move forward. It's important to take charge and know what you want to do and what you want to achieve personally, and in business, in order to increase success. Imagine your life and your achievements 10 years down the road. Make a picture dream board that you can display visually in your office so you can remind yourself daily of what you want to achieve. Make one side your personal dream board and the other your business dream board to inspire overall success.

Build a business plan that helps you to outline step by step and year by year how you will achieve your 10 year plan. Very few business owners actually make a plan and often sabotage their progress as they aren't focused on results and goals. They get absorbed as Technicians and Doers in their business, rather than being the Visionaries and Owners. A working interactive business plan with related action plans will go a long way to supporting your success. Start now!

Uncertain of your skills and impact? – Believe in yourself and your business impact. Too many of you undervalue the positive impact you have on the world around you; what you are worth to the world. Research has shown that most of us put a very low value on our worth and yet the world actually puts a higher value on our skills and impact. A test showed that if a job posting provided a salary of $50,000, thousands of people would apply. If the same job posting had a salary of $250,000, very few would apply. So why? Well, a lot of it has to do with our belief in our personal worth and our impact on the world.

So starting now, change your view of yourself. Believe that you are 'THE BEST' at what you do. Believe the service or product you provide is valuable to the world and that you owe it to the world to provide it to your customers. When you change this point of view, your perspective of your worth will change. A mentor of mine puts this very well, "if you believe in yourself and what you offer, and you believe in your product and service, you owe it others to provide that product and service to them, and help them buy it. If you don't believe in your offering, then you should not be offering it others." If you believe in yourself and value of your offerings to others, you will exude this in all you do. You should feel great about helping people with what you offer!

Take a moment to assess your beliefs in you and your offering. If you are not a believer yet, think about the above and what you need to do to make this shift. Do not be afraid to ask for help from others around you, you will be surprised at what you will learn.

Lacking Confidence that YOU are the best? – Learn to be Confident in yourself and your offerings. Confidence comes from a personal image you have of yourself and your impact. Confidence also comes from your life experiences and what you listen to from others. If others tell you to 'just be happy to have a job' and you internalize that, then your confidence will be restricted to that reality. But who can tell you what the future holds and what you can do if you apply yourself? Don't listen to nay sayers... Start listening to those around you who see your true potential and your true heart, including yourself.

Confidence starts with what YOU BELIEVE and what picture YOU paint for YOURSELF. Hmmm, so how do successful people do it? Successful people are very confident in themselves and their offerings. They embrace and internalize the beliefs in themselves and what they offer to others. They actually believe they owe it to the world to offer their products and services. This confidence becomes infectious and inspirational to others with whom you interact. It causes people to want what you have and to believe what you believe. This confidence is not arrogance or egotistical, but influential, motivational, and inspirational. If you have this confidence, it will come across in meetings with others and draw them to do business with you. If you do not, people you interact with will detect your uncertainty and be reluctant to do business with you. Have you been in a meeting and felt like something was off or you were reluctant to do business with this person? This 'feeling' is your reaction to their lack of confidence or commitment to themselves or their offerings. That lack of confidence may also be combined with a lack of belief in their offering or their sincerity. Combining it causes you to react adversely and decline to do business with that person.

Think about your confidence and your offerings. Close your eyes and envision the person you are and want to embrace — do this every day! Now assess your beliefs. Do you believe in yourself and your offerings? When you meet with others do you excite those you meet with or struggle to engage with them? Do you struggle to get others to work with you? Maybe you need to assess your confidence and commitment to yourself, what you offer, and the benefits to others. Ask others to provide feedback to you and what you offer. Ask them to tell you what they think you could do differently to help build the excitement. Build your new confidence plan first. You must believe in yourself and be confident in your skills and offerings. Ask for help if you need it!

Are you unhappy and "down" on life? – Focus on the Positive things, Positive people, and Positive life. Do you have people in life who are always complaining? Always blaming? Always down? Do you find it drains your energy and your excitement and goals? One of the biggest lessons I have learned is to surround myself with positive people who share the same passion to help others and who also want to have the biggest impact on the community that they can.

Have you ever been in a conversation with someone and felt like running away? Or, feel like as they spoke all the energy was draining from you? Those are the energy parasites. They are stuck in the negative universe and they zap energy from everyone they interact with, bringing them down. They aren't necessarily intentionally doing this, but they don't know any other way. When I am around these people I feel the energy drain and can't wait to run away and get into a positive space. Even though I feel sorry for these people, the reality is they have to make the change to the positive world themselves.

So why don't you help them by starting to change? Show them a different path by setting a new path for yourself. You can support them, but you can't change them. You can only focus on yourself, your impact, and your attitude and mindset. Make choices to focus on the positive and the future results. If something doesn't go right, then use it as a learning experience and focus on how to do or make it better next time. Don't beat yourself up over things that have happened, just focus on making a better choice next time. Focus on the Future not the Past, learn and grow! Use my definition of FEAR – Face Everything and RISE! Don't let bumps hold you back, use it to learn and grow forward!!

Are your choices and control of your time not balanced? – Learn to master choice making, managing your time usage, and control your POWER.

Many people make a series of choices that take them down a not so favourable path and they just keep making choices to reinforce that. Does this sound like you? Do you know that every time you make a choice, you have an opportunity to make a positive choice toward a different future? Really! You always have a choice, and each choice, big or small, leads to a new path toward your goals. Even if you have made bad or unfavourable choices you CAN turn it around. People who turn their lives around do this every day. They didn't have a miracle happen, they just started to make different and better choices. So let's start now.

Let's begin by looking at where you are now, how you spend your time, and what you are achieving. Then let's outline what you would like to be doing to spend your time and what you would like to achieve. Now, let's pick a smaller choice to start that you can use to practice making better choices. For example, let's say you want to start to appreciate your family more every day. Your first choice for change could be to find something to thank your family members for each day; watch the impact it will have on them. Another example might be to focus on one thing each day that you have achieved, add it to a journal of achievements, and make a choice to double those achievements each week.

Each time you face a choice, look at the two options and think about what you want to achieve in life and pick the one that drives you there. Don't pick what others would want you to pick or the easy way, pick the one that will move you toward your goals. I know that if you keep this up you will regain control of how and where you spend your time.

Now how do we put this all together ...

I know for many people they think these things are too simple and easy to have a massive impact, but reality is by using these simple steps above I have changed the direction of my life and I know others have done the same. What I experienced is that the little changes start to multiply and have a momentum effect. I started with the changes to the choices I made and then focused on being positive and future focused. I realized I had lots of people in my life who focused on the past and what they couldn't have and I had to start to surround myself with people who wanted to be successful and were more positive centred. Those two changes started a chain reaction. I also realized, as I look back, these two changes morphed into my confidence in myself and my impact on others, building confidence, plans, and dreams. From my experience, I know that I can help others to take charge, build confidence, and take control of building their business and personal success.

Want help? Ask me ...

Reflections

1.
What is the number one thing that impacts your future?

2.
What or who controls your future?

3.
To get the changes you want, what are the steps you are willing to take?

Cheryl Dyck
Senior Business & Executive
Coach, Speaker, Trainer

ActionCOACH
403.615.6440
cheryldyck@actioncoach.com
www.actioncoach.com/cheryldyck
LinkedIn: /in/cheryldyck
FB: /CoachCherylDyck

MENTORING
WOMEN LEADERS

Christine Till

The Marketing Mentress

This vivacious, enthusiastic, and intelligent entrepreneur, Christine Till, has 20+ years of management and marketing experience in corporate business and the healthcare field. She is a noted public speaker and hosts a radio 'podcasting' show dealing with social media and business marketing. She brings to your modern business theatre a wealth of knowledge, experience, and expertise in marketing using Linkedin.

Mentorship Through LinkedIn

Christine Till

Who'd have thought a cowgirl could be teaching social media in today's world?

Very early in my life, while studying to be a teacher, it became apparent I had a flair for sales and marketing. As time evolved, I was able to bring the two together, first through owning my own ranching operation, then through a successful real estate career, and most recently as a business consultant with a local college program for small business owners.

Through all these experiences, two key aspects have remained: being teachable and increasing sales.

I have been involved with business since the dawn of the electronic information age, when our civilization began using computers as tools not only to gather information, but also to increase connectivity.

Through the years, as connectivity has increased, most traditional sales and marketing systems have remained "hands on". It has only been in the last 5-10 years that we have seen a transition to the use of online systems, beginning with email marketing and then moving forward to even more modern platforms like Facebook, Twitter, and LinkedIn.

It is LinkedIn that I am addressing here.

I know you will find this interesting: *73% of my LinkedIn connections are male.*

For many years I've wondered why that was. Then I discovered two things:

1. Women are busy keeping multiple things on the go all at the same time. They are working on their businesses, raising their

families, helping their aging parents, volunteering, taking courses, and the list goes on. Women need to understand the importance of LinkedIn before they will make the time for it.

2. Most of them have started their businesses on a shoestring and they do not have the funding for yet another project that will not pay for itself.

What they need to know is this: LinkedIn offers connectivity to key, targeted business clients at no cost to their business.

But how do you do that? How do you 'mine' LinkedIn for business without a paid platform?

It all began for me with a stubborn boss and a determination to prove that I knew what I was doing. (I didn't, but I had faith.) When I read the company research and saw that they were marketing to the wrong audience — their own market research proved that 73% of the time when their clients (seniors) made decisions, the kids were involved — and were usually the Boomer gals — I realized it was time for a BIG shift.

Where were these gals at 2:00 in the afternoon when my boss wanted me to give a presentation at a senior center? They certainly weren't in attendance. I knew it was time for that big shift. But knowing how to make the shift was the real challenge. My boss was refusing to pay for any time spent doing online marketing, so I had to prove to him (on my own nickel) how important it was that it get done.

And this sent me, virtually 'kicking and screaming' into the 21st Century.

In a single day, I set up all my basic platforms for social media . . . and my website. I also had all my systems for recording and editing my podcasts and my podcasting show up and running. I was ready to reach out to my target audience and to prove, coincidentally, that my boss was stuck in the 20th Century.

Within an hour of posting my very first podcast interview on Facebook, I had a response back from a gal who said, "Oh, my goodness! I had no idea there was something available to help me with my 95 year old Dad!" I now had proof where our target audience was at 2:00 in the afternoon. They were at work! And, on social media.

A couple of years later, when my boss and I decided finally to agree to disagree, it was a blessing that I had already been through the learning curve. I realized then I could help others who were being literally dragged into social media feeling like their very finite head would burst at any moment because they are trying to force infinite information into it.

Could this be you? News flash . . . this too shall pass!

Five Reasons Why You Need to Use LinkedIn

1. The average age of people on LinkedIn is 43 years. The people on this platform are more seasoned business people and able to make buying decisions. They know and understand the value of marketing their businesses online.

2. The average annual income of people on LinkedIn is $125K. (The average income of people on Facebook is around $22K.)

3. It is the most professional business platform on the internet. There is not another platform on the 'net' that is more professional than LinkedIn.

4. Everyone on LinkedIn is there looking for business. They want to do business. They are hungry.

5. The groups are the key. It is through the groups that you can reach out to people and 'connect without being connected'. This is your major source of online networking, and should be treated as such.

Let's walk you through the basics of starting your own LinkedIn neighbourhood:

The first step is to set up your personal profile page.

LinkedIn has certain criteria we must/need to follow, if we don't want to end up in 'LinkedIn Jail'. For instance, use a professional headshot of yourself, not you and your spouse, or your kids, or your logo or your favourite car or a lovely plant. Also, use your real name beside your headshot . . . no degrees attached. Your Education and Experience will show up automatically in your headline box. You simply arrange it in the order you wish.

Next, write thirteen words for your tag line directly below your name. This phrase needs to tell people how you can help them. Just saying CEO of XYZ Corporation will be redundant, because that will automatically show up in your listed experience. Your degrees will also show up automatically, so you do not list them anywhere else in your tagline or beside your name. Your description is just that. Thirteen words that describe you and how you can help others.

Your Summary is the next most important item. This is where the head hunters and business owners are going to look immediately after they read your headlines. They want to get a feeling about you, the 'who' and the 'why'. A great rule of thumb is to share what inspired you to start doing what you do. Then you can mix a little in about your 'what' and 'how'. I am amazed how many business people omit this section!

Think of it as being in the largest networking meeting in the world and that these are still human beings looking at your profile. They will buy into your "why" long before they will buy into what you sell and how it works.

Your personal profile page is crucial to your success on LinkedIn. If you want people to take you seriously, you need to be as professional as possible on this platform . . . and just a bit transparent. I have interviewed HR managers with Microsoft, Amazon, and key hospitals. They all tell me that when they receive a resume today, the first thing they do is check the applicant out on LinkedIn.

Make sure they find what you want them to see!

Once you start getting active on LinkedIn — reaching out to communicate with people, sharing your material with them, or asking for their help with your projects — the first thing they will do is check on you by visiting your profile.

My profile has been crucial to people deciding whether or not to connect with me. I have had people stand up in networking meetings after they have heard me introduce myself and comment that, because of my profile and who they saw in my LinkedIn world, they decided to connect.

At this point, you will be reaching out to connect with people. Your goal is to connect with all the people you know first. If you cannot find them on LinkedIn, you can still invite them to connect with you if you have their email address. So, check out all your contact lists and copy all the emails. Put them into the special 'Invite All' window and hit 'send'. LinkedIn will do the rest for you.

Remember, only invite people you know to connect with you. Did you know that you only need to have five people say they don't know you and your LinkedIn profile gets sent to 'LinkedIn Jail'!? It is called being 'I.D.K'd' (I don't know you). Yikes.

Once you have set up your personal profile page, and if you are in business, you can set up your 'Company Page' — you need a company page. It works much the same as Facebook, only slicker. When you write and publish a new post on your home page or profile page, it automatically gets posted on your company page, your profile page, and your home page all at the same time. How cool is that!

All this can be managed on the free platform of LinkedIn.

But now, I'll tell you about the true secret to LinkedIn.

The groups.

You can join up to 50 groups. I know that sounds daunting, but you don't join to be active on all those discussion threads. You pick only a couple with which to interact. The rest, you set up NOT to receive emails and simply use them for mining. A rule of thumb is to join groups that have your potential market in them and that have ten thousand or more members. It will give you plenty of inventory when you start to do your searches to target your market.

It is here, in the groups, that you can connect without being connected.

LinkedIn is awesome once you begin to understand it and how to use it to the max. People who do get 60-80% of their business through this platform. It is where you will build the lasting relationships you need and want for business.

But there is another key that nobody thinks to teach . . .

You build the relationships online, but real business gets done offline. At some point, you have to bring your serious relationships to a face-to-face. We are gregarious and need to feel a sense of the other person, whether we are working in a B2B or a B2C relationship. Remember we are all people and sensitive to the nuances of human interactions. As mentioned earlier, I first used LinkedIn to connect and to find people to interview on my show, targeting those who supplied products and services for seniors. I found it immensely useful. But LinkedIn is a high profile platform and very complicated. It can be very challenging for the experienced Facebook and Twitter experts. For someone who has never used any social media? Scary indeed.

So now, I'll tell you how I did it: I used a coach.

I simply could not have accomplished what I did without one. In fact, at one point, I had 4 different LinkedIn coaches.

Ironically, it is those with some social media experience who are the most difficult to convince they need a coach. The next time you meet one, ask if they are getting 60-80% of their business through LinkedIn. If not, there is your answer.

For those who are serious about business, LinkedIn is the platform you want to maximize. If you try to do it without a coach, I estimate it will take you ten times longer to make it pay for your business.

Within six months of plugging into my webinars and personalized one-on-one sessions, you will be able to get most of your business through LinkedIn.

Just do what I do.

Reflections

1.
Why you need 500+ connections on LinkedIn?

2.
What are the five reasons you need to be using LinkedIn?

3.
What does it mean to be I.D.K'd? What is a L.I.O.N.?

4.
Why should you use a coach with your LinkedIn marketing?

5.
What are the differences between LinkedIn, Facebook, and Twitter?

6.
How many groups can you join on LinkedIn? What size should they be and why?

MENTORING
WOMEN LEADERS

Donna McColl

Drawing on her diverse background in business, industry, government, and non-profit sectors, Donna McColl offers her expertise to help individuals and organizations achieve their business objectives and avoid the pitfalls of poor planning.

From no- and low-cost campaigns to million dollar multi-year budgets, Donna's strategic guidance ensures the time and effort her clients put into working with her to develop a proactive plan for their unique business concept pays them back very well.

When not engaged in planning social media, websites, and other strategic tools with and for her clients and favourite charities, Donna uses the time she saves for herself to enjoy rock/ice climbing, skiing, drawing, theatre, and especially the company of four fine men in her life, her husband and sons.

Corporate Communications

Donna McColl

"Any press is good press when it's consistent with your brand," wrote Yariv Rabinovitch. While this may be true, it also highlights the caution and foresight that small business owners must apply before they position themselves or their organization into a "conversation" in the public domain, whether through the content on the company website, a public speaking occasion or a post on social media.

If you are like most entrepreneurs, you have been communicating from the day you decided to establish your business, but odds are that's been in just two dimensions — securing investors and making sales. However, to communicate effectively and avoid the pitfalls of poorly managed messages you need a communications plan that takes a much broader perspective, one that will help you make informed decisions that take you closer to accomplishing your overall business goals.

For your communications to be effective and memorable you need to stay open to criticisms, comments, and suggestions of others. You want to hear their voices — that's what keeps you innovative, creative, and resilient as the modern marketplace makes rapid adjustments and as your business evolves. Your brand and how it's managed are critical, but your audience's opinions, needs and desires are more critical. For example, Communications ASKS: Who are your website users? What are their needs? How do they use your website? How could it be better?

Communication Certainties

A communications plan is not an end, but rather the means through which you can keep on top of the marketplace and anticipate/mitigate changes that will impact your business. To that end, it can help to start from the fundamental understanding that:

- People expect quick and convenient access to information.
- People want two-way communication — they want to be heard and acknowledged.
- There is a tipping point between too little and too much information.
- In the absence of information, people will make things up.

- You are competing for trust, not merely the sale of a specific product/service/solution.
- Your audiences (aka stakeholders) are the people who have influence on your company's ability to achieve its objectives.

Stakeholders you may not have considered in your client-focussed business plan would include: your banker, lawyer and accountant, your neighbour merchants in the strip mall, your networking colleagues, the people who support the charities you support, the friends and relatives of clients, thought leaders in your industry and community such as politicians, NGOs and researchers. **The bottom line is that not everyone sees the situation the same way.** While price for value is a critical path, unless the price differential is perceived as large, people will decide to do business with you (or not) because of what you say, how you say it, and when you say it.

Key Messages

The foundation for your business communication plan is key messages. This is because words have only the capacity for meaning — it is WHO and HOW they are delivered and WHO and HOW they are received that makes for communication. Whether you are selling a product, a service or, as is often the case in non-profits a behaviour change, your organization requires a solid set of key messages that describes the features, advantages, and benefits of your offers/solutions. Guidelines for writing key messages include:

- Key messages should be outwardly focused and address the question: Who cares and why? What two or three key points do you need your audience/stakeholder to understand – prioritize them.
- Develop one thought in each key message sentence and only between three and five on any given topic.
- A minimal amount of background may be included for context.
- Cover the facts, include stats, and ensure consistency across all platforms when using them.
- To test your key messages, say them out loud to yourself and/or someone unfamiliar with your operations and ask:
    - Are they short and snappy?
    - Do they roll off the tongue? (i.e., one-third instead of 30 per cent)?
    - Are they in active language rather than passive?

- o Are they in plain language? This means no industry jargon and no acronyms.
- o Are they conversational, meaning "written for the ear" and not f or the "eye"?

Get Those Key Messages Out

While often the first thing that comes to an entrepreneur's mind (after financing), marketing is not the pinnacle of business communications, it is merely a subset. It is a one-way form of communication, and typically it is exposure you have to pay for (advertising, sponsorships) to make a direct link between consumers and demand. In marketing, the objective is to have a target audience respond to a call to action, such as "buy me", "try us" or "donate now".

Public relations, however, is the art of communicating with your stakeholders (including sales prospects) without selling. This means that rather than pitching your products or services, your business delivers relevant information that makes your audience feel more knowledgeable and confident in their own decision making. By becoming a reliable, trusted resource you can anticipate being rewarded with brand loyalty. This concept underlies why social media and content marketing (self-prepared copy on websites, for example) are the shiny new tools attracting the attention of businesses and marketers.

Sound public relations is also essential to reducing conflict, improving cooperation, and leveraging your marketing dollars. These goals may be achieved by tapping in to topics of public interest to increase awareness and understanding of your business offerings. It requires you to read and follow industry, business, and community news to identify what topics are newsworthy and which "beats" reporters and columnists cover. They are looking to inform their readers of the latest issues and trends and explain their meaning, you want to help them to do so, and in the doing become a trusted spokesperson. That said…

What's news to you and your company is not necessarily newsworthy.

General tips for dealing with the media

It's important to recognize that the same technology that spreads breaking news around the world in minutes has changed the way your local news agencies function. Traditional media is no longer about "breaking news" but rather the focus is adding value and depth to the seven-second sound bite that announced the incident or event in the news. As such, traditional media outlets tend to report not just the news, but the reaction to the news, and the reaction to the reaction. It is the impact on people that makes the story, otherwise known as the human interest angle.

Despite the high volume of searchable information sources available on line today, news media, in the traditional sense, is still held to be four to six times more credible than content marketing. This is why a savvy entrepreneur plans for both cold calls from reporters who seek the business out for comment on a specific topic and for proactive public relations that invite the media to the door under a deliberate strategy.

To begin, read and follow industry, business, and community news to identify what topics are newsworthy and which "beats" reporters and columnists cover. Then share appropriate content, and offer relatable comment on their articles and blogs. Until you reach out to them, these individuals they may not know you can contribute to the topics they cover. Then, pitch your stories to the most welcoming ears and/or pitch your expertise as a future RESOURCE for them — just remember that reporters a) are under no obligation to use your input, and b) nothing is OFF the Record - even when you are called for background information rather than a quote.

Reporters are always working towards a deadline, and there are two things they always need, visuals and quotes. In many cases, the first to provide them will be the source cited in the article, so be quick and be generous. It's a smart move to keep a file of original, high definition images as a photo/video library and develop pre-approved quotes based on your KMs to offer on behalf of your approved company spokesperson, which can help position your company's message in a favourable light. Even better, don't blow your own horn if somebody else will do it for you — ask your supporters for preapproved quotes to use in your own materials (website, news release, speech) and provide media with contact information for third-party verification. A good reporter always aims to provide readers with varying perspectives — why not make it easy for them?

Your goal is to help meet the journalist's needs. Feel free to say "I don't know, but I will find out for you". Ask for their deadline — and meet it. If you cannot contribute to the topic of interest, connect the reporter with other people who can and you'll be one step closer to building a good working relationship with that journalist.

Even the most exciting story won't get to the public domain if you don't pitch it to the right reporters. As mentioned earlier, finding them is a critical path in your public relations efforts. When you have a story to tell, use a news release style to capture all the necessary information — whether to be mass distributed or a one-of sent to a specific reporter after your telephone pitch. A public relations professional can help you be strategic with your timing, style the "news hook", employ your key messages well and ensure they are generated in the right format.

The following etiquette tips for dealing with reporters may help you become more comfortable doing so:

- Reporters are not trying to HOOK YOU; they are trying to inform their audience. Be polite, be professional, be authentic, be truthful, and be helpful. You may even ask for a do-over if you stumble on a recorded quote as they want their readers/viewers/listeners to get value from the story.
- Don't ignore small, specialized, regional or student publications, bloggers, etc. Be available—even when busy. Their stories may "have legs" that prompt much larger media outlets to contact you.
- Whether you were called for a quote or initiated a story, do not pre-empt a reporter's story. Upon publication/broadcast you are free to share it with all your stakeholders via email, Twitter, your website, etc. Until then, keep your enthusiasm to yourself.

Finally, recognize that assignment editors at print and broadcast outlets get hundreds of news releases and information bulletins a day. Breaking news at home or abroad will always bump you. Just remember you are establishing media credibility for the long term: if you have a message that has to get out for this weekend your only guarantee of timing is to buy an advertisement.

Reflections

1.
In addition to my ideal client, who else needs to know about the features, advantages, and benefits of what I offer the marketplace?

2.
Do I read/listen/follow the media outlets and reporters who cover topics my audiences are interested in?

3.
If I had a seven-second sound bite on the news what would I say about my business? What if I had two?

communications

MENTORING
WOMEN LEADERS

Mary Lou Gutscher

Mary Lou Gutscher has operated her own successful businesses for over 30 years. Her enterprises have included retail, fundraising, telemarketing, and a client newsletter publishing business that she grew to $1.8 million before selling to a jealous competitor.

Her work as a client and an assistant coach with Dan Sullivan, The Strategic Coach, led her to develop her own unique style of coaching as a valuable service for owners of small businesses. She has coached and mentored thousands of clients and is proud to share tips on one of the most important skills a business owner can develop — networking.

NETWORKING & REFERRALS: THE LOW-COST WORD-OF-MOUTH ROAD TO SUCCESS

Mary Lou Gutscher

Are you tired of wasting money on advertising and marketing ideas that do not work? Want a better way to build your business? Then it's time to get back to the basics and start connecting with people instead of waiting for them to call you.

Your first step is to follow up with your existing clients and those prospects most likely to need your services in the near future. Beyond that, you will need to meet people you don't already know. Here is a plan for you to do just that:

A. START NETWORKING

Since at any point in time, only about 3% of your target market is actively looking for what you have to offer, it is quite rare to attend a networking event and walk away with a sale, or even a referral. So why bother attending these business networking events?

Dorothy Briggs, **the sponsor** of this book often says: "Miracles happen when you show up!"

Goal # 1: **Initiate New Relationships.**

Each business networking event puts you in front of dozens of other business people, many of whom you might not have met any other way. You choose who to talk to while you're there and who to follow up with after the event.

Goal # 2: **Strengthen Existing Relationships.**

Whether it's a wave across the room, a handshake, a hug, or a quick question about what's been happening since you last met, being "present" for those you already know and like is important. Remember that 3% who might be actively looking for what you have to offer? That's where this comes into play. My largest and longest-term client came to me that way, as well as over 35% of my new clients in the past two years. That's part of the "miracle" I mentioned.

Goal # 3: **Identify Potential Referral Buddies**.

Your low-cost, word-of-mouth, referral-based marketing strategy is all about building a team of people who will act as your sales force. When you walk into a business networking event, pause and remind yourself of this fact: *Everyone in this room knows, on average, at least 250 other people!*

People want to know, like, and trust those they do business with, and the fast-track to being known, liked, and trusted is through referrals.

Once you've identified good referral buddies, you will have to train them and be trained by them to understand what to look for in a potential referral for each other. More on that on my website at **MagneticBusinessSolutions.com.**

Other Side Benefits

- It gets you out of the office. Running a business is a lonely job with the buck stopping at your desk every time. Having a chance to connect with other business owners, share stories and tips, and exchange information energizes you. It broadens your knowledge of what's going on in your city, town or region.

- You might find reliable suppliers there. How many times have you had to buy, fix or replace something and didn't know who to call? Remember the 250 people each of your network buddies knows? Call one of the Connectors in the group — often the organizer — and ask who they know who might help you. Easy, breezy.

- There may be opportunities to showcase your products, services, and expertise. While it's bad form and counter-productive to "pitch" your business in networking conversations, organizers often require speakers, and may offer the opportunity for a display table at their events. If either of these is part of your marketing strategy (and public speaking should be), networking groups provide leverage for you.

B. CHOOSE WHO YOU WANT TO MEET

At any networking event, you will want to keep your eyes open for three kinds of people:

- Potential clients — those who closely match your Ideal Client Profile
- Centres of Influence — those who influence the decisions of others you want to meet
- Potential Referral Buddies — those whose clients are similar to yours and whose products and services are compatible with the ones you offer

Start by identifying your **Ideal Client Profile.** Make a list of your top 10 clients (or the ones you would like to have). Write down what demographic and psychographic characteristics they have in common. This describes their occupation, age, gender, marital status, location, etc. and the wants, needs, or pain points they might have when it's time to do business with you.

C. DECIDE WHERE TO MEET THEM

Find groups that consist of primarily those individuals who fit the description of your Ideal Client Profile. Better yet, meet other business professionals who serve the same markets as you do. This provides the multiplier effect that cultivating Centres of Influence and Referral Buddies can produce for you.

Ask your clients where they get together with others like themselves and what other suppliers they work with. This gives you a starting list of possible organizations and groups whose events you might want to attend. If your clients are happy with your service, ask them how you might be favourably introduced to *their* friends or clients.

Below is a short list of other business networking groups and there are many more across the country.

1. Your local Chamber of Commerce is a good place to start. Chamber.ca.
2. Meetup.com provides an online networking forum that facilitates in-person meetings. If you don't find a suitable group in your area, you can always start one.

3. BNI – Business Networking International – has chapters in most provinces and openings to start new chapters. BNI provides training and structure for groups of business people who meet weekly and exchange referrals. BNICanada.ca.
4. Other local and regional groups exist, as well. For example, in the Edmonton and Calgary areas there are several monthly Womanition Connect Groups as well as larger Womanition conferences held several times a year. Womanition.com.
5. eWomen Network has chapters in several provinces and US States. eWomenNetwork.com.

D. MASTER THE ART OF NETWORKING

"You can have everything in life you want, if you will just help enough other people get what they want." Zig Ziglar

Before you can help anyone else, you need to know what they want or need. That's why it's important to get to know the other person first. People will get to know, like, and trust you quicker when you show a genuine interest in them.

THE FIRST IMPRESSIONS TRUST BUILDER™

1. Let The Other Person Be The First To Speak
"What do you do?" is likely the first question you'll be asked at a business networking event. Instead of giving your spiel, just answer generally then flip the conversation back to the other person. *"I do a bit of business coaching. How about you?"*

2. Ask Good Questions
The greatest gift you can give a person is the opportunity for them to be seen and heard. Since the context here is business, you might start by asking what motivated them to start their own business or choose their current career. *"What is your proudest achievement? What is your biggest challenge? What kind of clients do you work with and how do you help them?"* You get the idea. Be sincerely interested in what they have to say. (Read *"It's Not About You"* by Bob Burg & John David Mann.)

3. Give Relevant Responses
When it's eventually your turn, respond by referring back to what has already been said and, when appropriate, tie that in with examples of the work you do for your clients.

4. Ask How You Can Help

By being a good listener first, instead of being a pitchy salesperson, you become a source of support, a problem solver, someone who understands and wants to help. Ask the question: *"How might I help you in your business?"* Listen for the answer before asking permission to offer any suggestions of your own.

5. Be The First To Offer Referrals

When you meet someone with whom you believe you could form a mutually beneficial relationship, arrange a coffee meeting or a meeting at their office to learn more about their business and share a bit more about yours. *Givers Gain:* That's the motto of Business Networking International and, in some form or another, virtually every business networking group around. Once you know enough about the other person to know what some of their wants, needs, and pain points are, you take the first step and offer to keep your eyes and ears open for referrals for them, whether it is for a good supplier they may need, a good book, or an introduction to someone you think might require their services.

6. Develop Good Habits

Pick up your free eBook *"What To Do Before, During and After a Networking Event"* at MagneticBusinessSolutions.com. Then practice, practice, practice.

E. KEEP IN TOUCH

Networking is about initiating new relationships and strengthening existing ones. To build a relationship requires much more frequent interaction. Statistics show that *80% of sales are made on the fifth to twelfth contact.* If you want to succeed, you must follow up.

- **Start with a good Customer Relations Management (CRM) System.** This is where you keep your master list of contacts, categorize them and schedule your contacts according to how you have qualified them. I use Act! for my master database, which connects through Outlook for email and makes it easy for me to track and export to Constant Contact, my email marketing system, those contacts who've given permission to be added to my newsletter list. With the new Canadian Anti-Spam Legislation (CASL), permission becomes a necessity if you don't want to risk being reported as a spammer and suffer fines and system shut-downs as a penalty.

If you don't have special CRM software, you may want to start with an Excel spreadsheet. You can add columns and rows easily to replicate the fields in a CRM, and you can use the Comments feature in Excel to make notes. I've heard that Outlook's Business Manager can also work, but because I already have my own setup, I haven't investigated that.

- **Build Your Permission-Based Contact List**. Whether you have a newsletter now or not, get the okay to add contact information to your permission-based email list for future communication. I use the backs of business cards to have my contacts initial their permission to do that and offer a free eBook as a thank you.

- **Add Value With Every Interaction.** Purposeful communication with an education-based marketing mindset is the best way to do that. A newsletter, tips and ideas, or simply passing on articles of interest once in a while are ways to offer one-way communication.

  If you email a personal note, make sure your subject line tells them specifically what your message is about.

  When calling someone, I prefer to get to the reason for your call right away with little or no idle chit-chat. I recommend the same for you. Business people have enough time-wasting interruptions in their business day as it is, and you don't want to be one of them.

- **A Word About On-Line Networking.** The same general rules apply. When it is time to speak to someone in person, rather than sending them to an appointment booking website or on-line store, for example, then exchange email and phone information through messaging on line and continue to follow up. Post onto your social media profile, any tidbits that you might otherwise email, and learn the basics about following and sharing.

- **Bottom Line:** I've often heard that getting ahead is all about Who You Know. A word-of-mouth strategy that includes networking and referrals goes beyond that. It's all about Who Knows You. So set a target to become the Go-To Person for your contacts – the one who can connect them to what they want or need at any time. Celebrate the opportunities to help others because that's what keeps you front of mind when the time is right for them to do business with you.

For further tools and tips, please visit my website: MagneticBusinessSolutions.com where you'll also find my other contact information.

Meanwhile, Happy Networking!

Reflections

1.
Create an Ideal Client Profile by writing down what your top clients have in common.

2.
Show up where your top clients and others like them get together.

3.
Recruit, qualify, and train a team of Referral Buddies whose clients are similar to yours and whose products and services complement yours.

4.
Cultivate Centres of Influence who can recommend you as someone to trust.

5.
Provide referrals for others first. Refer often.

6.
Become the "Go-To" person by offering help and introductions wherever you can.

7.
Add value with every interaction.

MENTORING
WOMEN LEADERS

Rita-Anne Fuss

Sales dynamo, Rita-anne Fuss has turned her delight in fashion jewellery into a formidable network marketing empire, as her top sales recognition awards will attest; 27 Swarovski Crystal pineapples signifying number one sales in the country…27 times!

Partnering in the business with her husband, Curtis, this charismatic self-starter follows her passion bringing the joy of Fifth Avenue Jewellery Collection into the homes of countless women, while, at the same time, expertly empowering her extensive sales team to follow in her footsteps. Her famous motto is "ASK! ASK! ASK!"

Yes, just ask, because if you don't, how will you ever get the sale?

DREAM BIG – Your Destiny Awaits

Rita-anne Fuss

Growing up as an only child wasn't always easy, especially since my family moved fourteen times! Fortunately, my loving parents were such a positive influence in my life, teaching me to embrace change, to fearlessly try new things, and to always find the positive in every situation.

During my high school years, we lived on a farm, but, just before twelfth grade, yet another move meant yet another adjustment: new city, new friends. I learned how to adapt quickly so I could easily fit in to new environments, an ability that has always proved beneficial.

The one constant was my piano studies. Upon finishing, I even taught lessons myself, but in my later teens, I was ready to take some real risks, experience true adventure. I was seventeen when I had my first skydiving experience. Again, I credit my parents' wonderful, open-minded support in signing the underage waiver. Following my desire to "fly high", by the time I was eighteen, I had my pilot's license.

After graduation, I began working with autistic, behaviour and hearing impaired children as a special needs assistant with the separate school board. Clearly my childhood travels had left me with a thirst for new horizons, prompting me to take deferred salary leave and backpack on my own for four months through Hawaii, Australia, New Zealand, Fiji, and the Cook Islands. On my twenty-third birthday I was in Cairns, Australia flying in a glider doing loops and barrel rolls! I am currently a Lieutenant with the Reserve and, while working with Army and Air Cadets, I received a Gold Duke of Edinburgh Award from Prince Phillip.

A whole quarter century old, I married my wonderful husband, Curtis, the love of my life, and just three months later, we chanced upon what was to become our life's work, and certainly my biggest passion. Yes, that's when we heard about a Moose Jaw, Saskatchewan based company called Fifth Avenue Collection – Beautiful Jewellery. Hosting the jewellery shows together as a team taught us patience and mutual respect that served us well in the business and also strengthened our marriage.

My devoted parents had instilled in me a strong work ethic. My dedication and perseverance in getting the job done not only defines who I am today, but is also one of the main reasons why I'm a successful saleswoman.

Working with Fifth Avenue helped me expand even further as a person, giving me the opportunity to focus more on others instead of just myself. The company gave me all that gorgeous jewellery to sell, developing my marketing skills, as well as honing my mentoring expertise, as I trained my growing team to become business owners in their own right.

My joy in my new career path was somewhat overshadowed, however, when my mother suddenly passed away. Creating a positive opportunity out of an unfortunate situation, my husband and I sold our home and traveled with my father in his motor home for three months, selling our beautiful fashion pieces as we went, all across Canada right through to Newfoundland. Those jewellery sales paid for our entire trip! We had an amazing holiday doing what we love, essentially getting paid for having fun.

To me it is yet another indication of what I've always believed, that every moment in my life has had a purpose; everything that's happened to me was literally "meant to be". I am especially grateful for my children who continually inspire me to be the best I can be.

We've traveled as a family to countless exotic places in over forty-five different countries; more than half of these amazing trips paid for by Fifth Avenue Collection, in recognition of our superlative sales and mentoring. One outstanding vacation was in the Philippines where we met our foster child, and visited with a Filipino family for an entire month.

People will often ask me how long I've been selling jewellery. When I respond it's been over twenty-seven years, they can't believe it. I can't believe it! For me, it feels like no time has passed at all. I enjoy every moment because I truly love what I do. I seem to be quite good at it, too, as our Crown Jewel of Sales and Leadership will attest, not to mention our twenty-seven Swarovski Crystal pineapples, awarded to us for number one sales in Canada.

My experiences over the years have taught me a lot about living and loving life. It's essential to maintain that ongoing balance, keeping in harmony with business, family, and friends. Being a successful entrepreneur definitely has its perks — the ability to make your own hours and avoid rush hour traffic on morning and evening commutes. We've burned our mortgage and are now debt free. My extended success in a home-based business for all these years has taught me many lessons I'd like to share.

DIRECTION AND PURPOSE

Goal setting. The term gets tossed around a lot in business today. Truth is it's not enough just to formulate your goals in your mind. By actually writing out the game plan by which you'll realize your dreams, you FOCUS your intentions, and make a COMMITMENT with yourself. Of course, the next step is following through.

ESTABLISH A DAILY ROUTINE

You've defined your long-term goals. Now see each day as a mini version of your ultimate plan of action. You need to be organized, with a daily/weekly schedule and a written checklist outlining the tasks you intend to complete. This way you'll enjoy the benefits of getting more accomplished in a day.

MEDITATE OR PRAY

Living in such a busy world, we tend to get caught up in all the frenzy. It's essential to carve out some quiet time for yourself, moments of solitude you can devote to prayer or meditation. Maintaining a gratitude journal, faithfully recording the things that inspire you to give thanks will help you focus on your blessings, the things you've already accomplished, instead of everything you still want to do.

CHANGE IS GOOD

Don't be afraid of change. There is always a higher reason for it to happen in your life, a purpose you may not see right at the moment. Perhaps you won't like making the change at first, but once you're accustomed to the new, you usually come to realize everything was definitely for the best.

DRESS FOR SUCCESS

As a businesswoman, you are your livelihood. When you go out in your daily routine, dress up and look sharp as if you're in a professional environment. You just never know whom you might meet during your day.

BE PREPARED

Have your product and information in your vehicle ready to go at all times. Again, you never know whom you might meet, but you'll have everything you need to turn them into your next new customer. The more prepared you are, the easier it is to make the sale.

STEP OUT OF YOUR COMFORT ZONE

Refuse to let fear hold you back when faced with new things. Take a chance. Just go for it! The more you step out of your comfort zone, the further you will progress in your business, and in your life. Listen to that inner voice encouraging you to try. Take that first step.

DON'T TAKE "NO" PERSONALLY
When you ask for the sale the first time, usually the initial refusal is because they don't have enough information. You need to ask at least five times in different ways, from different perspectives. Trust me, if you don't, someone else will. Refusal is not rejection; you never know what the other person is going through at the time. Follow through and follow up.

LISTEN MORE, TALK LESS
Ask the questions, but spend more time listening to the answers. Not only will you come to better understand your customer and their needs, but, as well, you'll appear empathetic and approachable. The more likable you are, the more comfortable they'll feel around you.

SHARE YOUR STORY
When mentoring others to succeed in their own business, one of the most effective and inspirational tools you have is the story of your own journey. Share your experiences, your victories, as well as your setbacks, so they don't feel alone in the face of adversity. When others hear the extraordinary benefits the business has brought you, it'll encourage them to think that if she can do it, so can I!

BUILD YOUR CONFIDENCE
Celebrate your accomplishments, even the smallest of successes! As your business builds, so will your confidence. Focus always on the positive, and remember, your self-worth directly affects your net worth!

FREEDOM OF TIME
Running your own business, you have the flexibility to follow up on certain opportunities people working regular hours would be forced to pass up. For example, we've taken a couple of months off a year to just enjoy traveling. Take the time to pursue whatever brings you joy. It shouldn't always be all about work.

BELIEVE IN YOURSELF AND VISUALIZE
Have faith in yourself. You can do it! How would you use an extra $5,000 a month? Visualize it in every exact detail. See yourself as the success you are. Envision yourself already where you want to be.

SELF-CELEBRATION OR SELF-SABOTAGE?
What kind of language do you use with yourself? Would you say the same things to your best friend, to your beloved daughter? If you're self-sabotaging with negative head trash, then you're really holding yourself back. You need to reassure yourself repeatedly that you're beautiful, a unique, wonderful person! Learn to love yourself! Immediately turn any negative comment that slips out into a positive one. Over time you'll improve your self-image, and come to know yourself as the incredible being you truly are!

DO YOU FOLLOW-UP?
You would never ignore potential customers, yet how many times have you received a lead, or a referral, and never got around to contacting them? It is of utmost importance to always follow up. Maintain a log to keep track of the timing and content of your conversation then it'll be much easier when you contact them again.

MAINTAIN A POSTIVE ATTITUDE
Did you know it's been proven that happy people live longer lives? So put a smile on your face! It's easy to get caught up in all the negativity, but bottom line, life is a choice. You're in control as to whether you choose to have a good day, or a bad day, or an absolutely fantastic day. It's really all up to YOU!

DON'T BLAME OTHERS
In the end, "the buck really does stop here". You're the one responsible for your actions and their consequences. Five years from now, if you haven't achieved the level of success you desire, it's a choice YOU have made. If you want to be something different, you have to do something different. Make the necessary changes. Start today. Become accountable. Don't blame others for the way you are.

ASK! ASK! ASK!
This has always been my motto. If you do just this one thing, you'll be successful in your business. The more you ASK, the less missed opportunities. The more you ASK, the easier it gets. If you don't ASK, how will you get the sale?

STOP MAKING EXCUSES

What do you have to do to ensure the next twelve months will be the best year of your life? Write it all down. Read your list every day. Make a plan of action to have an amazing life!

TAKE ACTION

Do you want to feel empowered, self-confident? Do you want to change your life? Reading this is one thing, but you need to take steps, to do something every day to make it happen. You CAN do it! I wish you all the success on your journey.

My greatest pleasure is mentoring others to grow and change where they are today into where they want to be tomorrow. I can help you find your purpose and make your dreams a reality! You'll never know until you try.

DREAM BIG and never give up…until you find your Destiny.

Reflections

1.
If you look back at your life what risks would you have taken to step out of your comfort zone?

2.
What would be your dream job or career and what's stopping you from doing it?

3.
If you could change something in your past what would be different today?

4.
Where do you see yourself 5 or 10 years from now?

Zandra Bell

Zandra Bell minds YOUR business. A nationally acclaimed motivational humorist, this award-winning wordsmith is renowned on the corporate scene for creating original, inspirational hilarity customized to clients' workplace challenges and business objectives.

Designed to empower staff and increase employee engagement, these innovative keynote presentations, performed in the persona of her iconic comedy alter ego, stress management expert, "Shirley Best", are the ultimate solution to resolving workplace stress, and raising workplace morale and productivity.

A multi-talented "business revitalization" mentor, as well, very much in demand in entrepreneurial circles for her ingenious "empire building" and unique marketing savvy, Zandra is simply "creativity" personified!

Shine On Crazy Diamond

by Zandra Bell

Humour is a divine gift bestowed upon humankind to help us cope, to ease our passage through life's painful challenges. Fortunately, it's less expensive than alcohol.

I used to take for granted I had an ability to make others laugh, a sense of humour I'd honed to protect the real me, flawed and unlovable, from the uncaring world. Now I realize it's sublime, my power over the words, my talent for combining them thoughtfully, artfully enough to raise people up from the prosaic; to change their perspectives, inspire them to see things in an optimistic light, especially in today's stressful modern workplace. You scratch my back. I'll stab yours.

I understand now I am the ultimate healer, the silver-tongued diplomat; a clever court jester, masking intelligence with irony, crazy like a fox. I am a Leader, living by my wits and my words, my vocation to touch the hearts and the imagination of the populace, and thereby improve the world.

It only took fifty years to figure this out.

I wasn't quite five years old when I determined it was best to leave home, a tricky proposition since I hadn't yet learned to cross roads. Packing up my essentials — cookies, crayons and my drawing pad. I was a prolific creator of colourful, abundantly "animal-populated" landscapes in which I could imaginatively insert myself and exist therein. I set out unnoticed. I was often unnoticed, no doubt why I was leaving home.

Oh, they fed me. Mom was very big on canned food. I had no idea spaghetti started out hard. They saw to my welfare, but they didn't "get" me, and I certainly didn't "get" them. The circumstances of my birth to this couple, my parents, I suspected even then had to be some kind of colossal cosmic blunder.

I prided myself on my independence venturing out alone that first time, eventually settling down to do some drawing hidden in a faraway field of tall grass, which was, in reality, at the end of the block. With night approaching, it was time to seek shelter. Hmm…hadn't thought of that, but I knew my Gramma's house was somewhere not too long a "car ride" away, across a BIG road, near a major hospital.

The BIG road was almost my undoing. I have vivid memories of headlights right at eye level screeching to a stop, as I hurled myself out into traffic, running at top speed, knowing no other way in my innocence but to just get it over with as fast as possible, while hoping for the best. Now I think of it, I approached losing my virginity that same way, but that's definitely another tale.

I'm afraid my story ends rather anti-climatically, actually in both regards. After all my efforts, my traitorous grandmother immediately contacted my parents! I was sentenced to live with them another fifteen years. Fifteen more years of the inanities and insanities, the miscommunication, the thin veneer of outward normalcy masking the hopeless futility Pink Floyd describes so succinctly as, "...hanging on in quiet desperation is the English way".

They weren't really bad, although Mother definitely had her eccentricities. She'd never answer the door...not even for us. The doorbell would ring, and our dog would burst into endless high-pitched barking. So would my mother. "Why do I always have to answer the door? Why me? How do I even know who it is?" The visitor would eventually just go away. I never knew what Girl Guide cookies were till adulthood.

It's hard to describe exactly why life with them made my brain explode. My parents went every Friday to the Scottish club. One such night, with my mother out of earshot, Dad leaned over and thanked me for coming, confiding that he really didn't enjoy himself, but only went every Friday because my mother loved the bingo. Later, while my father was up replenishing our drinks, my mother expressed her delight in my company because Fridays were usually so boring, but "Your father just loves that bingo". Just think, week after week after week. They were a familial version of Chinese water torture.

The bathroom was another land mine of dysfunction as Mother was mortally afraid of the toilet overflowing. Used tissue, a potential culprit, was to be placed in little strategically placed paper bags. Flushing was verboten, prior to her inspection and approval. This seemed to be contradictory to the way others handled scatological matters, so, as a child visiting people's homes, I was usually so paralyzed with fear of being punished for not doing it "right", that I would procrastinate so long it would end in incontinence, and I would get the strap anyway, or the fly swatter on my inner thighs. I was very "bad" and very "selfish".

School became my salvation. Obedient, artistic, intelligent, creative, I was a celebrated A-plus student fawned over by faculty, invited to read my creative writing stories over the PA system every morning. Naturally, all the other kids hated me. They jeered at my weight, and my weirdness. I learned not to shine so brightly…in self-defense.

Entering high school, I determined to make a change. With no outside help and clearly no knowledge, I decided to lose weight simply by ceasing to eat. It worked. Soon I was a successful anorexic exercising hours a day. When I couldn't fight the urge to eat, I added bulimia to my repertoire. Even though I was eventually down to just over a hundred pounds, this all escaped my parents' attention.

By university, I was rising at dawn to do two hundred sit-ups and leg lunges before my classes. I'd return home for more intense calisthenics, before work at my part time job, followed by a late night run, encouraged by my ever-supportive father. "I don't know why you go to all this trouble. You'll always be fat. You'll always have the 'Bell' bottom."

I was driven. I've always been driven. I so excelled academically that, in my graduating year, one of my professors told me I shouldn't bother submitting my last few essays because "I could teach the class." I had such low self-esteem it took me years to really appreciate how intensely complementary that was. He called me Mademoiselle Bell, l'Originelle, "The Original One". I had such brilliance, but it was almost all obliterated. Such power, but I gave it all away.

We all have upsets, tragedies, seemingly negative setbacks woven into our lives, forcing us to make difficult decisions and take action. It's how we learn, and grow to understand the Universe. Every single thing you experience is meant to be happening in your life at that exact time, everything unfolding for a higher reason. Far from being a mistake, it was divine purpose that I was born in my family. They were meant to drive me insane. My "assignment" is to love them anyway, to transcend all the unworthiness that my upbringing instilled in me, and to succeed in my quest to fulfill my true potential by first learning to love myself.

Continuing to achieve, in six years and three cities, I went from part-time federal government worker to youngest regional director in my department in Canada. My bureaucratic phase was a mind numbing, soul-destroying experience actually quite similar to living with my family, but at least this torture paid.

Then again, if I hadn't been so unfulfilled, if I hadn't ended up with a deranged, tyrannical meglomaniac boss, I would never have capitalized on my talent for comedy. One of my erstwhile mentors had insisted I couldn't make it without the regular government pay cheques, not being the "starving artist" type. True.

So I innovated a whole new approach to motivational speaking, entwining comedy into the corporate workplace, customizing humour designed to reduce stress, raise morale, inspire employee engagement and, thus, increase staff productivity for a better company bottom line.

Who says an artist has to starve?

My hilarious alter ego, "Shirley Best", quickly became the "toast of the town", garnering rave reviews at popular arts festivals and traveling to key note engagements all over North America, comedy royalty on the conference scene. Twice voted Funniest Edmontonian, honoured as a Global Television Woman of Vision, at one point, I was on the cover of three prominent local publications at the same time! Celebrity status meant countless media spots, including the local TV station shooting their morning show out of my luxury condo to promote one of my upcoming stage shows, their camera wires trailing down eleven floors.

It was fabulous! Just like my university professor's homage, however, it wasn't really hitting home. I was embracing it all. Grateful for it all, I definitely wanted it to continue, except for a tiny, niggling misgiving. What if everyone realized I was an imposter? Not an incredibly talented star at all, just the bad, selfish, fat, undeserving, neglected little girl, who tried so desperately to get her parents to notice her, to love her, to no avail. Everyone enthused I was so smart and funny, so why didn't I have my own TV show? I was seeking bigger, better speaking opportunities. Why was my career only going so far when I wanted so much more?

Of course, you could always count on my dear father to say just the right thing. "You know what your problem is, Zandra? You have all these hopes and dreams. The sooner you realize you'll never be anything more than you are now, the happier you'll be." I knew he came from a place of love for me, smothered in his own fear granted, but love nonetheless.

As always, I had to go it alone.

I forged on for years doing my absolute best to be the absolute best. I may not have had everything I wanted, but I had a fantastic life...until my mother died, my father had to have a serious operation, and somehow I ended up becoming his caregiver! Never was there more unlikely a "geriatric whisperer" than I, no matter how dedicated, continually commuting between two provinces on a bi-weekly basis as he aged, a situation that not only compromised my freedom, decimated my finances, but also plunged me back into the inanities of my dysfunctional family, and the stagnant desperation of my childhood. The crab's claw of responsibility had pulled me back down into the bucket.

There were depressing times through the thick of it all where I had to face my deepest fears, and resourcefully struggle just to survive. On the outside, my career never faltered. Inside however, I was undergoing one of the most transformational experiences of my lifetime, new and deeper understandings blossoming in their divine timing. My personal ordeal served as a catalyst, forcing me to question life, and dig deep within for answers. Eventually truth, honesty, and I triumphed and, surprisingly, I realized that my father had become a treasured friend.

Endlessly striving to make oneself happier on the inside by searching for something on the outside is like a manx cat chasing its tail. Everything you want...success, abundance, love...it's your birthright, already right there in front of you waiting for you to get out of your own way. Realizing your dreams is not an acquisitive "reaching for" process, but more of an exercise in "excavating" requiring you to remove all those blocks you've piled in the way, the pain, the disappointment, the negative messages of undeserving and unworthiness you've sadly conserved and unconsciously believed all these years. You have to unclog your pathway to self-love, the true key to having it all.

In the past, even though I wanted more, worked towards more, I could never have more. Not because I didn't deserve it. Of course, I deserved it! We all deserve the best. It was because I didn't BELIEVE I deserved it. Now I know I do.

Opportunities are opening up effortlessly before me now as I continue to explore new horizons, empowering my corporate audiences through my customized humour, learning more life lessons along the way.

Most recently, combining my wordsmithing talents and speaking experience with my unique marketing inspirations, I've begun mentoring other entrepreneurs in the art of "creative business revitalization", sharing intriguing insights that owners are often too close to their business to realize. In essence, it's all about creating your niche, your business "empire", and then effectively utilizing the right words in the right way to compel your potential clients to choose YOU, your products, your services. Your passion and my imagination together…the possibilities are endless!!!

The wise Marianne Williamson says that "our deepest fear is not that we are inadequate", but that we are "powerful beyond measure", our "light" being the aspect that "most frightens us."

My beloved father passed away last week, and I vow, in his memory, to never dim MY light again due to fear and self-doubt, but to SHINE brightly, unabashed, in all my God-given glory, while encouraging others to do the same.

Look out world! Here I come, Zandra Bell, l'Originelle.

Reflections

1.
What negative messages about yourself were instilled in you during your upbringing and early life experience?

2.
Are you still harbouring these outmoded beliefs from your past?

3.
Can you see certain aspects of your current life where these limiting ideas could be holding you back from achieving your goals?

MENTORING
WOMEN LEADERS

Grow Yourself

Cyndy Morin
Darlene Schindel
Deborah Kurach
Deborah Nichol
DK Beitel
Eva Shaw
Lil Lezarre
Pam McCormack
Sam Rafoss
Sandra Fisher
Shirley Borrelli

Cyndy Morin

Cyndy Morin (BA Psych with distinction, LLB) practices Family Law with Resolve Legal Group, winner of the 2014 International Legal Awards for Best in Family Law and Nominee for the 2015 National Philanthropy Day: Generosity of Spirit Award. Prior to her legal career, Cyndy was a counsellor working with families and youth. It is from this background that Cyndy developed a unique holistic systems approach to best serve her Family Law clients. Cyndy sits on the Canadian Bar Association Access to Justice Committee and teaches law courses through a joint initiative between Chinook College and the Alberta Law Foundation.

Evolution of the Best Laid Plans: A Personal and Professional Journey

Cyndy Morin

"Life is what happens when you are busy making other plans" – John Lennon.

The year was 1994, and I was pregnant with our first child. My common law partner and I settled in Calgary, Alberta and had our lives all planned out. We decided we would have two children, and he would be the sole income earner from his contracting business, while I stayed at home to be a fulltime mom. The plan was to grow our own fresh food, never let our children taste McDonalds, or be in the care of a third party. We had it all figured out. Our son was born in 1994, and our daughter was born in 1996. And the plan was all was going well, but was about to change in 1997.

In 1997 we learned we were expecting a third child, a daughter. Not quite what we planned, but a worthwhile deviation from the original, and a pleasant surprise, nonetheless. She was due on my partner's birthday, March 22, 1998, and we were both very excited to meet her. But then, on December 2nd, 1997 my partner was tragically taken from us in a car accident while coming home from work, and the well thought out plan for our lives completely changed in an instant. Family and friends rallied around me, with love and support, to get me through my loss. But, once everyone returned to their own lives and the reality of the uncertainty before me started to set in, so did fear.

In addition to being devastated from the loss of my partner, I was terrified about my future. I was 27 years old, with a 3 year old son, an 18 month old daughter, and one more on the way. I only had a grade 10 education, I was unemployed, and hadn't worked outside of the home for some time. Then, there was the fact that not many employers would be eager to hire a 6 month pregnant woman with two other babies at home. To make matters even more challenging, one of my children was diagnosed with autism and, with that, came the need for speech therapy, occupational therapy, and a whole host of other expenses I was not prepared for and did not have the money to pay for.

I was definitely at a crossroad. I had to make a choice to go on welfare or do something different. I chose the latter, even though I did not know at that time what path that would be.

Dealing with urgent obstacles

First, I needed money. Although I wasn't crazy about the idea of going back to school, I did know that it was probably a necessary evil. More importantly, I could obtain a student loan that would inject a temporary cash flow in my direction until I could figure out my next move and look for work. The student loan would also help me establish my own credit rating and get some services in place for my autistic child. Going back to school felt intimidating, but I also felt some strange solace to have at least a pointed direction to move toward. Some sort of future, albeit uncertain, a future of sorts, nonetheless.

Growth does not happen in isolation.

During this time, my sister, Dr. Corrina Iampen, completed medical school in Saskatoon, and decided to move to Calgary. I didn't realize it at the time, but my sister and friend was about to also become my mentor and one of the biggest supporters along my journey. She arrived in Calgary, started her own clinic, and I watched her grow her own medical practice. My sister offered her direct support by financially assisting me throughout my initial hurdles. She was always present with words of encouragement, the occasional kick in the behind, and she would cheer me on with every small achievement. In addition to this direct support, through my observation of her own achievements, she vicariously instilled in me the value that with hard work and perseverance I, too, would be able to reach my goals. In fact, not reaching my goals was never an option; it wasn't a question of "could I?" it was a question of "how?" The answer to the question of "how" came from my own curiosity and inquiries about other people's journeys toward success. I started questioning people who I felt were successful, either professionally and/or personally. "How did you get to where you are at?" Like my sister, hard work and perseverance were common traits among the individuals to whom I spoke. The following is a list of additional themes that appeared to be a common denominator for success:

- View obstacles as opportunities for growth and learning.
- Seek out and accept the support of others.
- Keep momentum, continue to move forward.
- It's not what you know, it's not even who you know, it's how you network.Never underestimate the importance of fostering and maintaining positive relationships with others.
- Surround yourself around positive people who add value to your life and reciprocate.

- Be confident, be bold, and be grateful.
- Never compromise on your values.
- Create the vision of where you want to be. Focus on your end goal, but be flexible enough to change the goal, if needed.
- Find a mentor, even if it is someone you don't know personally – maybe a respected professional in your field, and emulate them.
- In addition to emulating your mentor, discover your own unique gifts to add.
- Don't "think" you can make it, "know" you can.
- Be willing to build up and support others. Pay it forward.

All of these values apply equally to both personal and professional growth goals.

Application of the Common Denominator

After the birth of my youngest daughter, I found a few part time jobs that I could work between classes. The original plan to have a life of growing my own food and having children never knowing the taste of fast food or third party childcare was thrown to the wayside. We were in survival mode and daycares and McDonalds became the norm. And that was okay, because I did what I needed to do to continue to move forward. Dwelling on what "could have been," or on the guilt of feeding deep fried chicken fingers to my children instead of broccoli would only divert my focus of moving through what was a temporary path.

Even the dread of going back to school soon subsided as I started to become inspired through my education. It took me two years of changing my major multiple times within a liberal arts program before I realized I had a true passion for psychology. I discovered I wanted a career where I could help people through their own difficulties and achieve better outcomes. I used my major in psychology as an outlet to also learn more about the treatment of autism. My research led me to Autism Calgary, which was a parent run organization, where I met some incredible parents who mentored me about the different avenues of treatment I could explore with my own child.

I had entered this world of unknowns with my education and the development of my children and, in particular, my one autistic child, but through the support system of mentors, those unknown worlds became familiar and manageable. I could never have created and ran the in-home early intervention program I put together for my child without the mentorship, guidance, and support of other parents who lived the experience before me. It was primarily from that experience that I learned the importance of seeking out support. I realized there is no need to attempt to do things on your own. There are individuals willing to share their time and knowledge with you, and it is important to accept help when offered. Once I realized the benefit of this, my world really started to expand and open up.

A New Approach to an Age Old Profession

After earning my Bachelor of Arts Degree in Psychology with Distinction, I applied to graduate school in psychology, but also to law school as my "back up" plan. I didn't really want to be a lawyer, but I also didn't want to put all of my academic eggs in one basket. It turned out to be a good call, because I didn't get into graduate studies; however, I was accepted to law school. The "new plan" was to attend law school and then eventually get back into psychology. Once again, that plan fell to the wayside, and I allowed myself the flexibility to change my focus. I realized I could still have a career where I was able to help people through their own difficulties to achieve better outcomes — through the practice of Family Law.

After completing law school and articles I went to go to work for a prestigious Family Law Firm where I began to develop my skills as a lawyer. However, during my time there I found several of my clients were under such stress and grief that they had difficulty just coping on a daily basis much less having the focus or ability to make sound legal decisions. For example, despite giving the best possible legal advice, sometimes clients would sign agreements because they were exhausted with the process or out of money, instead of signing based on their own legal entitlements or desired outcomes. Ethically, I felt more supports were required for family clients above and beyond the legal services being provided. Traditional law firms focus only on legal matters, particularly when lawyers cannot bill for any work outside of legal services. After working within a traditional framework for 5 years at my firm, I began to feel restless and felt there was a better way to deliver family law services to clients that were more aligned with my values. After mustering up enough confidence, I decided to take a brave leap. I left the firm to open my own, Resolve Legal Group. Before leaving, however, I sought out the advice of a lawyer friend of mine, Jeff Kahane, who owns his own firm. Jeff gave me much needed insight that helped me efficiently and effectively set up my practice allowing a smooth transition for my clients.

Opening my own firm afforded me the ability to create a unique way to address family matters from a client centred, holistic approach. This means, in addition to addressing a client's legal matter, I could also bridge families with differing community supports based on individual need. Our firm achieves this by having on staff a fulltime "Client Support Coordinator". The Client Support Coordinator follows up with our clients, at no additional cost, to connect them with whatever additional supports they need to help them through what can be one of the most difficult times in their lives. It is my philosophy that with the right supports, clients become empowered to make sound legal decisions when files are led to resolution. The response from our clients about our approach has been tremendously positive as demonstrated by our rapid growth. Resolve Legal Group's humble beginnings in 2011 consisted of me as a sole practitioner with one assistant, and within a year the firm grew to 10 staff. By 2014, our firm expanded to two full service branches, our original office in central Calgary, and a second firm on Centre Avenue in Cochrane. It is my desire to continue the firm's growth so that holistic practice becomes the norm in Family Law, rather than the exception.

The Power of Mentorship

Throughout the journey of opening my own firm, my sister has continued to be by my side offering both financial and emotional support. She encouraged me to continue with my passion. My friend, Jeff, has continued to be a mentor to me, as well, offering me business advice and assistance whenever I need it. Words cannot express how much their mentorship, guidance, and support has meant to me over the years.

It is because of the powerful mentors in my life, the families from Autism Calgary, the support of my sister Dr. Corrina Iampen, and dear friend, Jeff Kahane, and countless others that I can attribute part of my success in both my personal and professional life. It is also the reason why I now pay it forward by offering to mentor others with the knowledge I have to share. If I can offer any guidance, to you the reader, it would be this:

1. Seek out a mentor, someone you admire and someone who has the skills or know-how you wish to emulate.

2. Fear can be immobilizing — acknowledge it, but move through it — you really can overcome anything, it all boils down to simply making a choice.

3. No matter what, keep moving forward. Even if you are unsure of your ultimate direction, the end result will find you so long as you keep moving forward.

4. Be flexible. You may have a plan, but be willing to let it go if it doesn't work out the way you originally envisioned.

5. Let people help you. No successful person I have ever met, made it to where they are in isolation.

6. Be grateful, and always take the high road, no matter what.

7. Don't forget to look back at your own achievements and celebrate them.

8. Give back. Become a mentor yourself and be there for others who may need you in some way.

9. Be creative, do something unique and different that makes you stand out above the average.

10. There is no such thing as real failure, only divergence toward a different path if things don't work out on the one you are on.

You really can realize your vision.

Reflections

1.
What traits do the people you aspire to be like share?

2.
How do you show your gratitude to those who have helped you move forward toward your goals?

3.
How do you celebrate your own achievements?

4.
What fears do you have that are preventing you from reaching your desired goals?

5.
Think about what makes you unique to anyone else in your industry. What added value can you offer? How can you make a difference?

6.
In what positive ways can you cope with stressful situations in your life to get you through difficult times?

Darlene Schindel

Darlene Schindel is a Registered Nurse and Certified Transformational Leadership Coach, Mentor, and Speaker. Her nursing career has taken her from the bedside to the boardroom, working with all healthcare professionals. She was the 2013 Alberta Medical Association Medal of Honour recipient for non-physicians. Darlene is passionate about inspiring people to live their best life, fired up, and with full purpose. Being a mentor is a powerful part of inspiring others and a role that she embraces. Because of her love of nursing and the healthcare field, her work is dedicated to supporting deep transformational change for nurses at every level of the system.

Just Imagine...

Darlene Schindel

"One's destination is never a place, but rather a new way of looking at things."
Henry Miller

Things happen in life where we come to a cross roads, and in those moments our futures are often defined.

There have been many such moments in my life, not just the devastating or life and death situations that I have experienced, but challenges and opportunities that required I make a choice, a decision. Sometimes I knew exactly what I wanted – like the moment I met the most amazing man, fell deeply in love and knew I wanted to spend the rest of my life with him. That was 33 years ago and every day we are together I discover more and more what deep love really feels like. Other times, I was hurt, frustrated even devastated, humiliated and disappointed. But in all cases, as I reflect back upon them, what came of each situation was largely influenced by my perspective, the way I saw the situation, my values and my beliefs.

My career as a Registered Nurse has been amazing. Being a nurse was not something I grew up dreaming about. In fact, from the moment I finished Grade 9 and moved on to high school, the constant conversation at our dinner table was about what I was going to do with my life, I better decide, I better make it good, I better prepare for university. And all the while I was excited to go to school and go to Phys Ed, play volleyball, play basketball, any physical activity or sport (except for swimming – never loved it) was what was on my mind. I loved the team aspect and the natural high from being physically active. One spring, as I was crouched down on the track tying up my runners, I heard someone yell "heads up!" I looked up just in time to see the discus hit the ground and bounce up and graze the right side of my head above my right eye. Needless to say that was the end of that track season.

In reflection, I realize that what attracted me so much to sports was in large part due to a Phys Ed teacher who saw in me what I probably didn't see myself, and through her mentorship and belief in me, my abilities were nurtured, challenged, and supported. When I look back at it now, I see that there were also great teachers that mentored me in this same way in junior high school. I will always be grateful for their support and belief in me, when I hardly knew who I was.

At the end of high school, I was no farther ahead with making a life path choice than I had been at the beginning. I was dating a guy who I thought was the answer to life's choices, and so I turned down an opportunity to go to college on an athletic scholarship. I never told my parents about this. So not having made a decision about post-secondary education, I started looking for work. I found a full time job at a nursing home, as a care attendant. It was here that I met another highly influential mentor who affected my life path.

Shauna was a young Registered Psychiatric Nurse, who was the nurse in charge on the floor I worked on and my immediate supervisor. We had a pretty cool team of attendants, all mostly young women like myself, and the patients on our floor were the youngest in the nursing home, most with a variety of mental health issues. What made that job so attractive to me was the fact that Shauna had great energy and such an exuberant passion for her work and the people we cared for. She made us feel we mattered, she nurtured us by gathering us every day for 'rounds', not just to pass on the daily happenings to the evening shift, but to teach us about our patients, what their health issues were, what that meant in terms of why they responded or didn't respond to us, and how we could care for them in a way that would help them be at their best. I loved learning from her. She inspired me. Something about her drew me to the field of nursing in a way I had never even thought about before. I made a decision to apply to nursing school — and I got in!

The very first week of nursing school two lectures left a lasting impact on me. One was from our Registrar, a pleasant engaging women who told us that if we were sitting here in her class, committed to being the next Florence Nightingale, with blinders on, ready to move full steam ahead, then we better think again. Being the next Florence meant being a whole, well rounded person, who came to class, studied hard, but also took care of herself, had fun, was active and spent time making friends.Those words stuck with me always, and those of you who know me today, know how often I quote Aristotle — "the whole is greater than the sum of its parts."

We also had a lecture that first week from a senior obstetrician/gynecologist in the city. There we were, a room full of bright eyed young women, and he stood up saying that before our class graduated, three of us would be pregnant — you should have heard the gasps that preceded the hush that fell on the room! He went on to tell us that in his career he had delivered 10 virgins, and seeing some puzzled looks, our first anatomy lesson began!

When it came time to choose where I would start my nursing career, there were three areas that greatly attracted me — Emergency, Intensive Care, and Neurosurgery. Nursing school had provided many opportunities to practice and learn in a variety of settings, and it was in these areas I felt the most alive, challenged, and passionate. In my ICU rotation, I had an amazing instructor, a great teacher and mentor. Her 'job' was to teach us, but she had a much bigger effect on my life. Although never in a formal mentorship role, that is what she was for me. She brought something to life in me, ignited an interest, a passion that I hadn't been aware of. I have followed her career, and to this day, I connect with her to discuss ideas and get her opinion and wisdom.

I chose Neurosurgery. It was a perfect fit, with a small Neuro ICU, a step down or intermediate care area and the general ward. All the challenges and fast paced kind of work I loved was there. But that wasn't what drew me in. It was the nurses. As a student they taught me, and expected me to work as hard as they did, treating me like their equal. From them, I learned what it meant to be a caring, compassionate nurse. Here was another example of the power of mentorship, in an informal way.

Only four and a half years later, I was on the move, changing hospitals and making a leap to nursing management. This was a huge decision, but I knew I was ready. I now was in a position of formal authority and leadership. It was a time of transition, but also the beginning of transformational change, which at the time I probably did not even realize. Debbie Ford once wrote *"we all have the ability to be the catalyst for motivation or to play the part of a game-changer in the life of one another or many."* Now it was my turn to teach, lead, and mentor other nurses and health professionals within my circle.

One young nurse's story stands out for me, as a new graduate on her first job, Cheryl struggled with the role and the expectations. Neurosurgery is a demanding area to work in, both physically and mentally and certainly isn't a fit for every nurse. I struggled with Cheryl, too. She was pleasant enough and seemed to be trying, but as her three month probationary period came to a close, I was torn about how to handle the situation. It would have been easy to fail her, as many were suggesting I do, and let her go on her way, finding another place to work, and post her position for another nurse. I had to make a decision. I had to think differently and from somewhere other than what I saw superficially. I chose to give her another chance. I chose to believe that she had potential, more than she showed and that if

I invested in mentoring her, she could be a good nurse. I had to believe in myself, too. That gutsy choice proved to be the right one. Mentoring Cheryl was very rewarding for me. And Cheryl? Well, she became an amazing nurse, found her own path of leadership in trauma care, and went on to support and mentor many other nurses under her supervision.

From those early days, my journey continued along with my education. I completed a post RN Baccalaureate degree in Nursing, as well as a Master's Degree in Health Studies with a focus on Leadership. I chose this path because I was following my passion. Many people get stuck because they feel they don't know what their passion is, and that it has to make them feel like they are on fire inside. This is often not the case, in fact, we may have several passions. Think of them as things that are of great interest to you, what you are curious about, or inspires you, and from which you may experience many feelings: such as a deep sense of calm or inner peace, love, fulfillment, joy or just feeling complete.

My nursing career had been wildly fulfilling to me personally as well as professionally. I had worked with amazing healthcare professionals across the healthcare field, cared for patients and workers from the bedside to the board table, lived through great financial challenges in the system, always finding myself thinking about how we could do things better.

Government decisions in 2009 resulted in funding cuts (again) and my position was eliminated. What affected me most was the fact that the team of professionals I was working with at the time was devastated, as all the work we had done up to that point in redesign was now null and void, and I think we all felt devalued.

For me, I was at that crossroads, where I discovered the field of coaching, and embarked on a two year journey of study, self-awareness, and development that brought me to a whole new level of possibilities as a Certified Professional Coach. I could see vast opportunities to apply my new skill and practice in so many areas. Yet, I was always drawn back to the field of nursing, and with the support of my coach, realized that it was the nurses who I cared deeply about.

I believe that in healthcare, there is not one professional who is more valuable than another. Our greatest value to society is the whole care of the person, body, mind, heart, and spirit. We provide most value when all professionals work collectively and collaboratively across the continuum of care. This is a paradigm shift for many professionals, especially doctors. This is largely due to the nature of western health care education. However, my experience working closely with doctors was very different. I have experienced and been part of the possibility.

Making the shift to being a self-employed nurse, starting a business that would serve nurses on a path of self-development, self-care, using their voice and providing massive support in a way that is not currently experienced has uncovered my passion for possibilities and the power of transformation.

The key is CARE. Caring builds relationships inside organizations and with those people they serve. Nurses want their patients and clients to know they care about them, and this requires that the organization they work in has a caring culture, as well. Don't we all want to work with a company or organization we see as a partner or friend — with employees we enjoy working and interacting with? We want to work with organizations that meet our needs, help us grow and develop, and with people we respect and like. When you show someone you care, they care back, and you create strong relationships that lead to success.

There is a great shift underway in the world as we know it today, and I am committed to using my life to inspire all those who cross my path, to be ALIVE — living a life of PASSION, PURPOSE, and POSSIBILITIES! "The start to a better world is a belief that it is possible"- author unknown.

Nurses have great stories. You either are a nurse, you know a nurse or you have been cared for by a nurse, and in that context you have a story. In those stories lie the key to transformational change and the future of our healthcare system. I would love to hear your story.

Reflections

Winston Churchill said, "We make a living by what we get, we make a life by what we give." The most meaningful experiences people have in giving and making a contribution involve mentoring others. Interestingly, even being aware of this fact doesn't seem to affect how we choose to contribute in society, where we volunteer, projects we take on or even jobs we apply for. Brendon Burchard describes mentoring as "a responsibility and a privilege on the road of life." There is something magical that happens in a mentorship relationship, no matter what setting it is in.

Reflective practice is a powerful tool for not only our personal but also our professional lives. Take a few moments to focus on yourself, your needs and your life, your wants, needs and desires. Remember, working on yourself is the key to attracting new opportunities and affecting others.

1.
Am I clear on what I want or could I use support to figure this out?

2.
Will the choice I am making move me toward an inspiring future or will it keep me stuck in the past?

3.
Am I standing in my power or am I trying to please another?

4.
Will the opportunity I am considering guarantee my ability to mentor others?

MENTORING
WOMEN LEADERS

Deborah Kurach

Awarded by The Chamber of Commerce, Deborah Kurach received "The Most promising New Business" in 2001 and "Business of the Year" in 2007. Recognized as a business leader by the business community, Deborah has been decorated with numerous nominations and awards since she opened Verve Salon and Spa. Over the course of her entrepreneur career, her staff reaped the benefit of Deborah's passion for teaching, positioning her as a valued mentor with the Womantion Mentorship program. Dedication to community and several charities stem from her belief that honesty is a fundamental value, one that every business can, and should, be built upon.

Success is a Matter of Making Quality, Purposeful Decisions

Deborah Kurach

My vision for Verve Salon and Spa was cemented in my mind long before the shovels went in the ground. Verve is the result of a lifetime of learning, planning, and staying true to my vision and purpose.

An artist created the name "Verve" four years before the property was purchased. The plans were developed and we opened the doors in August 2001 with a dedicated staff of 25. Spas were limited in the Sherwood Park area 14 years ago. I set three priorities during the planning stage and wove them into the design and building plans. First and foremost, we had to be first class. A new business either has to be first to market or stand out as number one. Secondly, we understood the importance of location from the very beginning, and third, we had to provide free parking.

Setting goals and making change

I believe that when we are ready, truly ready, to make a change or improve areas of our lives, the tools and circumstances unveil themselves to give us what we want, but we still have to do the core work.

Setting goals is an interesting process. At the time of developing, planning, and writing out our goals, we envision what the end results may look like. As time goes on and events unfold to reveal the milestones along our path, accomplishments feel like every day life, there aren't any marching bands to greet us at the junction of a milestone. When we close the last chapter and attain what we set out to do, we look back to realize that we may have made it, but the rewards and accolades were evident in the pebbles and obstacles along the road.

Setting goals and reaching them takes a huge commitment and, for me, commitment to quality has defined the Verve brand since the day we opened. I believe that if we are to stay on top of the beauty industry, our clients should have access to the latest, most up to date services available. We spare no expense in training. We send staff members on courses and have contests to win trips to seminars and workshops around the world. I want my staff to be the best so our clients have the best.

The industry is very different than it was when I began my beauty career 20 years ago as a nail technician. Techniques were new and "unpolished" and I sensed even then the potential to improve the process, the quality and the level of hygiene. I made the conscious decision back then to raise the bar in the industry. Over the past 19 years, I have become an esthetician, permanent make-up artist, and licensed private educator. I am continuously taking courses to grow my knowledge base and I pass that knowledge on to my staff.

Verve is a chosen salon by exclusive product lines, such as Unite or Kevin Murphy, and we've been invited to special events in San Diego, Las Vegas, Mexico, including events at the Edmonton Art Gallery, and we like to share these experiences with our staff who have earned the privilege. After all, it is a privilege to be in the top 20% of salons that make the grade to carry the exclusive product lines; we have worked very hard to maintain a high standard in everything we do.

Adding a retail component to Verve was a natural fit for me after ten years of retail buying experience between 1988 and 1998. Clients love shopping at Verve and the eclectic assortment of products and gifts in the front of the salon has grown from 3% to 35% of our sales and our compliment of staff has growth from 40 to 50 over a 10 year period.

I was approached in 2011 to provide a weight loss program through Verve, complete with full training for my staff and myself — if I chose to take on another learning curve, and it was a steep curve. We decided to add the program and dedicated an entire area in the retail section on the main floor to the products that support the program and we included an area for consultation.

Over time, I watched as customers came in week after week to purchase their weight loss products or just to meet with their weight loss coach. I watched as each week passed and they were shrinking in dress sizes before my eyes. I knew the program was effective. I knew these women, they were my clients in other areas of Verve. I understood their struggle to shed their unwanted inches. Everyone had a story of their own to share, and I interviewed many in hopes to discover a common thread or trigger I could relate to, because I had my own secret wish to lose weight.

Fear of Failure

Many new and seasoned entrepreneurs will admit that fear of failure not only keeps them up some nights, but it can be a very powerful motivator to keep you moving when things are not going as planned. Moving through the fear and doing it anyway creates an environment for self-actualization.

In my personal life, I have recently accomplished one of the most difficult goals I have set for myself. In a five-month period, I lost a total of 50 lbs. What is so interesting to me is the plethora of benefits I have realized by reaching this goal. Along with the confidence, I have gained an incredible sense of freedom and insight.

When I made the decision to lose the weight, I told no one. Looking back as to why I kept it a secret, I learned that I had a fear of failure, one that most likely kept me from attempting this goal for so many years. A nagging doubt lay dormant for so long that when I made the commitment, I wanted to be sure I could do it before I told a soul. Now, when others ask me how I achieved my new look, I am proud to share the process; I have bragging rights.

Reaching weight loss milestones is a tangible success that can be measured on the scale and with a tape measure. When the pounds begin to melt away, many things begin to happen. On the outside, my clothes were loosening. I began to see the improvement in my skin and, on the inside, I was soaring. My confidence level exploded and I wanted to do more. Every pound urged me to the next pound and within five months, I had met my goal and lost a total of 50 lbs.

Now that I have cleansed my body of unhealthy foods and I am regularly taking the proper vitamins. My eye doctor confirmed that my eyesight has improved 50% since my last eye exam. I no longer need glasses, perhaps the program I am on has something to do with this, after all, it is the most significant change I have made since my last eye exam.

Years before I opened Verve, I knew what I wanted. My business purpose was to open a high-end salon and spa. Everything I did leading up to the opening day was to support that purpose. Being on purpose creates a natural flow in life. Being on purpose to lose 50 pounds had the same profound affect on all areas of my life, as did the milestones I marked in business.

In the book, "The Power of Habit" by Charles Duhigg, he talks about how changing one habit sets into motion a domino affect of positive habits reaching all aspects of a person's life. For me, losing 50 pounds has improved my relationships with my customers, we can now relate and share our successes. I have a lifestyle that makes health sense. I understand the quality of my food choices is just as important as the quality choices I make in my business to ensure success.

Reflections

1.
Is fear holding you back from being the very best you can be?

2.
What does quality and purpose mean to you?

3.
If there is one thing you could change about yourself, what would it be and why?

Deborah Nichol

Deborah is the director of Healing Heart™ Wellness, she's a Holistic Health Practitioner, Mentor, Writer, and Speaker.

As a Holistic Healer, Deborah works in conjunction with other health practitioners, such as Naturopaths, Osteopaths, and Chiropractors to help solve specific and challenging issues for their clients. When treatments hit a plateau, they are referred to Deborah to get to the root of the problem.

Her unique holistic training, intuitive abilities, compassion, integrity and sometimes a dash of humour, help people get to the core of what is energetically causing their health issues and consequently guides them to begin the healing process.

Love & Light,
Deborah xo

The Hidden Power of Your Life Story

Deborah Nichol

There's a hidden power in our life story. Our life story tells about our journey and about how we came to be who we are. All our mistakes and experiences reflect how we see the world. It's a beautiful, messy life and embracing that vulnerable part of ourselves allows others to do the same. Imagine a world where it was okay to make mistakes. Okay to feel the way you feel and okay to be whom you were meant to be, and you were loved for it. I invite you into my world, a world full of challenges and amazing life experiences, in the hope that together, we can discover the influence that our very existence has on one another.

So how do we find balance and live in harmony? First, we must know chaos and fear. And this my friends, is how you do everything the hard way. I had no idea there was an easier way and even if I did, for some reason, I feel the need to experience the things I most need to learn and have compassion for.

I got married in my early 20's to a man 11 years older than myself. We moved to a small town and, since there were only about 100 people in the town, getting a job was near impossible unless someone died. So what's a girl to do? I had a baby. It makes sense, right? I was away from family, friends and, although the ladies in the town took me under their wing, I was lonely. This was the start of the fear. We moved back to Calgary and had another baby, the good ideas just kept coming! So, here I am 23 years old with a newborn baby girl and a 16 month old little boy, a controlling husband, who didn't help out and an unhappy marriage. So what is a girl to do? Have an affair? So I went in search of someone else fixing my problem and making me feel good about myself and so begins the chaos…Wow, I found him, I actually knew him from high school (This would actually be my second husband, but I'm getting ahead of myself). Man, I tried everything to have an affair with this man, but to no avail. He told me that if I wanted to be with him then I would have to leave my marriage. So did I leave my marriage? No, I decided to have the affair with a mutual friend who was going through a divorce, and so the chaos grows. This was not stressful in the least. My life was full of little children, an unhappy husband, working at night, laundry, baths, cooking, cleaning, and an affair.

Things were going south, quickly. I was stressed out and started to take it out on my kids, something I promised I wouldn't do. So, off to counselling I went. I had been before when my parents got divorced so I felt comfortable to go and talk about my life, but leave out certain parts. Like how my husband was an ass or that I was having an affair, or that I felt like I was worthless and a terrible mother. No way was I going to tell anybody those things. But as life goes, you can only carry so much baggage before it catches up with you.

This particular day would change the course of my life forever. So just a couple of things you need to know about me before we get to the next part. At this place in my life I believe a few things about myself.

I have the worst luck ever, I am unlovable, I am in trouble and I can't tell anyone. What would they think? I have ruined my life and my kids' lives. Maybe it would be better if I wasn't around anymore. As I was driving all these overwhelming thoughts and feelings came. I thought about driving into the cement overpass, I accelerated and I was going to end all this pain and hopelessness. Instead, at the last minute, I had another thought, what if I don't die? What if I become a quadriplegic? That would be just my luck. I was too chicken to try to take my life. I couldn't even do that right.

When you ask if things can get any worse, the answer is always, yes. So on that fateful day when I arrived at counselling I was brave and told her about what happened on the way. I broke down, cried and just couldn't stop. So she took me to the Holy Cross Hospital and I was checked into the Mental Ward.

I was officially broken. I officially had a good understanding of Chaos and Fear.

Now started the search for balance and harmony, keeping in mind that I do things the hard way. You have to make certain promises when you end up in the hospital, you have to promise not to hurt yourself. You have to promise to continue therapy for a year.

I started my journey outside of my brokenness. I searched for understanding, love, acceptance, confidence, and worth. I started by moving in with my mom, with my 2 kids and my pregnant cat. You just can't make this stuff up. I got a divorce. This was a long tough battle, it challenged every part of me. I didn't have enough self-worth to do this for myself, but I sure could for my kids.

I continued counselling and I continued lying. What would she think about me if I told the whole truth? Now, I look back and can hardly understand my reasoning, everybody already knew I was broken. I had already shown that I was weak, and there was nothing worse I thought, than to have other people know that you are flawed.

Along my journey, I read as many self-help books as I could find. Then I met a dear friend who invited me to a spiritual workshop, she did all this soul work.

I was intrigued and so I went. On the lecture night this facilitator explained to everyone that, "everything we don't heal we pass on to our children." Omg! All I could think was "my kids are screwed." I started to cry. Just when I thought I couldn't mess my kids' lives up anymore, I learn this.

I was a single mom and couldn't afford to take the course, but my luck was changing. The lady who sat beside me had already signed up for the course and she had won the draw for a free weekend — she leaned over and gifted it to me!

That was over 22 years ago. When I first started my healing journey, it was because I wanted something better for my kids.

I wanted them to know they were loved, to feel it and share it with others. I wanted them to be confident and know who they are. I married the man I wanted to after all the chaos — we've been married for 20 years. It's been messy and hard and beautiful. He lets me be me, and he loves me. He is a wonderful dad to my children who he calls his own, and the two children who I thought were screwed, are amazing, compassionate young people. All of this. The hard way!

The key to enjoying our life is to embrace it all. All our flaws and weaknesses have lead us to this place, and this is the place you were meant to be. One simple premise in life that remains true is we need to know who we are. Taking your experiences and weaving them into your own life story is just as important as living and learning from them. Finding the lighter side of everything that has happened in my life, is how I make it okay. Otherwise, it would just be one screw up after another. Some may see it that way; however, I see it all, completely different.

I am so grateful that I have had such a grand learning curve in my life. If I had known self-worth I would have never gotten married at such a young age, or had children. I would have never admitted that I was broken and then I wouldn't have busted my ass trying to find myself. I would have never remarried and known what it was like to feel unconditionally loved. I wouldn't have been able to be who I was meant to be.

All of these things are part of finding your balance and your harmony, knowing who you are and being okay with it. You already possess all the inner wisdom, strength, and creativity needed to make all your dreams come true. It is hard for most of us to realize because the source of our unlimited personal power is buried so deeply beneath the excuses, the blame, the bills, and the chaos of what we call our daily life.

When we can't access our inner resources we come to the flawed conclusion that happiness and fulfillment come only from outside of us, or from others. When we rely on these external sources, and they do not give us what we need or they leave, they take our happiness and our sense of worth with them. Then we feel empty. When we rely on our knowing of who we are, we start to attract and create the life we want. We create the family, the job, and then, we live from a place of passion, fulfillment, and joy.

I will leave you with this, have the courage to tell your story with your whole heart — make the unknowns-known, do things that matter to you, navigate your strength, give the things you want most. We all impact one another's lives. Be authentic and real, laugh until tears run down your legs, let go of who you think you are and embrace who you are and say to yourself everyday "I am enough!"

Reflections

1.
It is never too late to discover who you are.
Who you are is important.

2.
You never know how sharing your life story will impact another.

3.
It is possible to go from broken to whole, all in the same lifetime.

4.
You make a difference.

DK Beitel

DK Beitel is a Registered Nurse, and more importantly, she helps people understand and have compassion for themselves as well as the people they love, play, and work with using Enneagram Personality Theory.

DK experienced a challenging childhood and used the Enneagram for her mental, emotional, and spiritual healing, as well as assisting her in parenting and professional growth. These experiences compelled her to become a Certified Enneagram Facilitator. She studied under Dr. David Daniels and Helen Palmer and was certified in Menlo Park, California in July 2010.

DK offers classes and workshops and is a writer and motivational speaker.

Turning Points: My Healing Journey with the Enneagram

DK Beitel

I grew up in a difficult home; filled with challenges and conflict. There was one unbreakable rule in my family: think, feel, and act as my parents did or suffer the consequences. There was no understanding or compassion for difference in my home. As a small child, I promised myself that when I grew up my life would be different.

My childhood experience set me on a life journey of wanting to understand myself and others with compassion. During my twenties I became a Registered Nurse, married and became a mother. In the course of my thirties I was divorced, became a single parent, and continued to work as a Registered Nurse. I also started my own practice as a Registered Massage Therapist and Reiki Practitioner. I have always been interested in a holistic approach to health and how we heal mentally, emotionally, physically, and spiritually.

Throughout my forties I faced several challenges. I decided to let go of my holistic practice and continued to work as a Registered Nurse. The greatest challenge I faced was being diagnosed with breast cancer at forty one. It started out with a quiet inner voice telling me to go for a mammogram. At first I ignored this advice by telling myself that I was too young for breast cancer, a short time later I had a nightmare in which a storm destroyed everything around me, which convinced me to book a doctor's appointment. Shortly after my mammogram, I received the phone call I had been dreading from my doctor's office requesting I come in to talk about my results. It was during this frightening wait between my initial diagnosis, lumpectomy and final pathology report that I had several major realizations that would change the course of my life. First, I realized how short and precious life was; until the diagnosis I had felt invincible and was certain I would live forever. I was understandably distressed about the idea of dying and leaving my young son behind. The second realization was that I had dreams that I had kept putting off, I kept thinking I would do them in the future. I had a few simple dreams — owning my own home, having a dog, and studying Buddhism. I suddenly realized that I might not have a future and it was heart breaking. I made myself the promise that if I lived I would go after my dreams.

As I successfully completed cancer treatment and healed, I created a dream list and faithfully pursued my dreams. I now have my own home, a Border collie lab named Frankie, and I am a student of Buddhism and am in good health. As the years have gone by, I have checked off the dreams I have accomplished and continue to add new dreams to my list. My dream list reminds me of how short and precious life is and that when I die I don't want to have any regrets for what I might have done or become.

The second challenge I faced was my son was growing up and I didn't know what I would do to fill this empty space. For a time I felt lost. I had spent a great deal of time and energy focusing on being a healthy and positive parent. All I knew is that I wanted to do something that I was passionate about.

After a great deal of searching and reflection, I realized I had always had a deep interest in understanding myself and others. Enneagram Personality Theory was introduced to me twenty years earlier by a mentor to help me understand myself, my ex-husband, and my son. I had just gone through a divorce, was facing the challenges of co-parenting, and I also wanted to look at the impact my childhood had on me. The system became an integral part of my personal and professional life and a vital part of my emotional, mental, and spiritual healing.

Enneagram Personality Theory is the study of 9 different types of people, each with their own perspective on the world and different ways of thinking, feeling, and acting. It is a system with spiritual and psychological elements, and relies on self-observation, self-reflection, and action for personal, spiritual and professional growth.

My childhood trauma had left me living with constant emotional, mental and spiritual pain. The Enneagram was one of the systems I used to heal from this pain. It allowed me to understand the core unconscious negative belief of my type, which added to my suffering; every type has their own core unconscious negative belief about themselves and the world which causes them to suffer. I am a Type Two: The Helper; and the belief of a Two is that we must give to be loved, not give in simple ways but give in big ways — including time, energy, attention and even money. It is not surprising that this core belief led me into nursing, as many Two's enter helping professions. This core belief contributed to my pattern of attention, which is watching for the needs, feelings, wants, and desires of others but ignoring my own. Knowing this allowed me to begin paying attention to my own needs, wants, feelings, and desires allowing me to heal. The Enneagram described the unconscious, habitual, and limiting emotional and mental patterns I developed to survive my childhood and how to change them; each type develops their own limiting emotional and mental patterns.

I didn't have healthy role models for parenting; the Enneagram was one of the tools that assisted me in being a positive and compassionate parent. As Elizabeth Wagele writes in her book, The Enneagram of Parenting (HarperOne publisher, 1997), the system allowed me to understand my son, who was a different type than I was, and allowed me to see my son's special talents and support his interests even though I didn't share all of them.

I have used this personality theory in my nursing career. As a Registered Nurse I have found myself in situations that are stressful for clients, colleagues, and myself. Thirty years ago, I was a nursing student on a busy surgical unit and a patient had stopped breathing. The Registered Nurse who found him started throwing large pieces of furniture across the room and yelling orders at the staff.

After the event the staff talked about how the patient had survived and they also marveled at the dramatic change in this Registered Nurse's behaviour. She was usually laid back and quiet and no one had ever seen her behave this way before. What I had witnessed, unknowingly, was someone moving into their stress patterns.

The Enneagram describes the stress patterns of different types. Each type finds different circumstances stressful and responds to stress in a variety of ways. I know these descriptions are accurate because I have been watching them play out in clients, colleagues, and myself for the past twenty years. Having this information has helped me manage my stress differently and have understanding and compassion for others when they move into their stress patterns.

This system also meets my values of understanding myself and others with compassion. For all these reasons, I realized that I believed in the power of this system to create positive change in people's lives and that I wanted to study Enneagram Personality Theory and to share it with others. I studied under Dr. David Daniels and Helen Palmer and became a Certified Enneagram Teacher in Menlo Park, California in July 2010.

Every type has their own set of challenges. As a Two, I find it difficult to ask for help, being an entrepreneur has made me even more aware of this. After a few years of trying to do everything on my own, I began to ask for support in the areas that were not in my scope of knowledge as a Registered Nurse. My son has become my technology guru, I now have a business consultant who has assisted me in creating a business plan, marketing and promoting. I also receive financial advice from an accountant and financial planner. My business motto has become "ASK FOR HELP"; each type will face their own particular road blocks as an entrepreneur.

Every type has their own set of gifts. As a Two, my most comfortable position is behind others supporting them. This is one of the gifts of my type and it has allowed me to be a good mother and Registered Nurse.

One of my challenges as a Two is being the center of attention and sharing who I am, this is extremely anxiety producing and I have a fear of being rejected. Each type has their own specific fear which can paralyze them and stop them from moving forward in their life.

When I first certified to teach the Enneagram five years ago, I was terrified of standing in front of others and sharing the Enneagram. I used several strategies to get me through my fear. The first strategy I used, and still use, is talking to myself with compassion, reassuring myself that I can do whatever is in front of me. The second approach was that I practiced speaking in front of people and leading workshops whenever I could, no matter how big or small the group.

These simple, yet courageous strategies, have transformed my life and I have discovered my love of motivational speaking, facilitating workshops, and writing. When I do these things I know I am living my passion because every cell in my body wakes up and shines and I am filled with energy.

As I have shared the Enneagram, one of the challenges I have encountered is dealing with negative people. When I first began to teach, a friend of mine attended a presentation and after the event gave me brutal feedback. At first I was devastated and took her criticisms to heart. I began to question whether I should be teaching the Enneagram despite the fact that this was my dream and I was passionate about it. Then I remembered the core negative belief of my type, which is that to be loved, I have to give to others and be approved of. Once I was remembered this and reminded myself that I was loveable, despite what other people thought of me, my pain began to

ease. Every type has a core believe which causes suffering in their life.
I made a conscious decision to ask for help and talked with several trusted mentors about this distressing situation. This gave me another perspective on the situation and continued to lesson my distress. I continue to learn that asking for help, as difficult as it is, consistently changes my life for the better. It allows me to change and move forward to build a brighter and more fulfilling life.

In the end, I decided to let go of the friendship. I realized I needed people around me who supported my dreams and who were kind, positive, and compassionate. I have learnt that I need to protect myself from people who, consciously or unconsciously, trample on my spirit and my dreams.

This situation was another turning point for me, I could have crumbled under the weight of this person's brutality, but instead I made a decision. I promised myself I would not let others' opinions, disapproval, or negativity control me. This gives me courage every time I am about to facilitate a class or workshop, write or speak. It allows me to keep the promise I made myself thirteen years ago, after living through breast cancer, that I would pursue my dreams.

When people ask me what I do, I say ,"I work as a Registered Nurse and, more importantly, I help people to understand and have compassion for themselves and the people they love, play, and work with using Enneagram Personality Theory."

Reflections

1.
What challenges have you overcome in your life?

2.
Where in your life are you able to ask for help? How does this feel?

3.
Where in your life do you have difficulty asking for help? How does this feel?

4.
What have been the turning points in your life? What have you learned from them?

5.
What promises have you made to yourself? What has it meant to keep them?

6.
What dreams do you have? How are you pursuing them?

MENTORING
WOMEN LEADERS

Eva Shaw

Eva L. Shaw, Ph.D., is a registered clinical counsellor and leadership trainer. Always persevering, she is a woman of character and high esteem with the ability to eloquently convey ideas.

Leadership training is an investment in oneself to accomplish life's greatest goals. Combined with the transparency of life experience and formal education, Eva's passion is mentoring women who dream big and want guidance to accomplish their dreams! The exceptional gifts of empathy and teaching come from an outpouring of who she is on the inside. Her entrepreneurial abilities are phenomenal.

Eva Shaw - Makes Life Happen!

Women Who Persevere ACHIEVE Their Dreams!

Eva Shaw

Will you persevere? My definition of leadership is a continuous learning from within that creates and promotes success.

Make Life Happen is an expressive title for my business. I coined it when contemplating my history of over 25 years experience in the field of social work and clinical counselling, including my personal journey of failures and successes.

The mission is to teach and walk beside those who have the desire to mature spiritually, emotionally, and physically. You must be motivated and want to benefit from my expertise and knowledge. Through this relationship, I will share my wisdom and experiences as a life leadership woman in small business. Let's build our dreams together!

What is perseverance? One definition I identify with is "courage stretched out". It is about enduring and overcoming difficult circumstances with hope and joy. If we don't learn to persevere through struggles, we will simply give up. When we persevere, until we come out the other side, we grow stronger and we develop greater confidence. Leadership is not for the faint of heart.

We are women of great value, unique in our own way and each of us is a masterpiece. We are the elite of the elite and we are high achievers. In my personal achievement of meaningful success, I have been blessed with expert mentors who taught me well. This challenging path to success will transform your life. Are you ready to reach your highest potential?

My own business! I am fired up and full of vim and vigor. When the initial elated thoughts of freedom, flexibility and being your own boss wane, you may enter a time of worry. Most things we worry about will never happen, so when we worry, we are wasting our time and emotional energy for nothing. Let's ask ourselves the question. "Is what I am thinking pushing me forward to live out my dream?" If the answer is "No" then change that thought!

What about disappointment? It will come. Perhaps, other people in our network of friends don't believe in our dream. We may not get the support we are hoping for from them. When disappointments come, there may be

"What if?" questions that lead to regret, or we may put blame on others. Neither of these responses are appropriate and can lead to discouragement, resentment, anger, shame or bitterness. If, however, disappointment is seen as an opportunity to learn and grow, or if we choose to focus on what we can change and not on what we expect, we can view disappointment from the proper perspective. Life is full of disappointment. Let's dwell on what can be, not on what could have been. We must determine to grow through the experience. We must stay focused on our dreams. This is a great time to look at the PLAN for the business again, ADJUST what needs to change, LEARN and then DO what has been learned.

My Personal History

At the tender age of seven years, making life happen became a reality when I was diagnosed with Type 1 diabetes. I lived on a farm with my family in Ontario where my father was a farmer and my mother was a stay at home mom. It wasn't expected that I would live a long life. The prognosis was not a good one and it changed my family dynamics considerably. My mother was an example to me as my first mentor. She persevered through these very difficult times and taught me through the years how to be a successful diabetic. There was little written about diabetes then and my mother searched and researched everything she could find. There also were no computers to help her. This is where I began to learn to have perseverance, strength, patience, and determination to live well. My dream was to have the same chance in life that my friends were experiencing. I continue to count each and every day a blessing and a gift.

Medical doctors were advising me not to have children and I endured many lectures. But I had a dream, I met the challenges and I have two amazing and healthy sons. I am thankful for the progressive medical and technical resources to treat diabetes today and I am an insulin pump user. My greatest struggle in life has been living with diabetes. It is never easy and to date there is no cure.

I loved being a stay at home mom, but when divorce became a reality I was forced to change direction, build a career and persue post-secondary education. My dream became a doctoral degree in counselling, which I achieved as a mature student while working full time. My next dream was to cross the stage to accept my doctorate degree with no student debt. It was a struggle and quite the story, but I did it.

A couple of years ago I fell and broke my femur bone. It was a life changing experience. Due to diabetes, I have peripheral nerve damage in my legs. Between the two, I can no longer walk long distances. The hidden disability is now visible for all to see.

My career has included positions in retail, not for profit and corporate organizations; self-employment, entrepreneur, executive management and front line positions. Much of my career has been working with women and their issues. Society's expectations of women sometimes brings fear, insecurity, guilt, blame, anger; low self-esteem, self-image, and self-worth issues. After all, we must be an amazing partner, super mom, as well as successful in a career and beautiful at all times.

Two awards for my accomplishments are: The Joslin Diabetes Centre, Boston, Massachusetts, U.S.A Award for 50 courageous years living with Type 1 diabetes and The Visions of Excellence Award, Coquitlam, B.C. for perseverance in developing a small business. These awards remind me to continue to be on fire, every day, for my life dreams.

Presently, I am a self-employed business woman and joint entrepreneur with my husband who is a school teacher. We enjoy LIFE! I professionally counsel women who are struggling with therapy issues. A few issues are sexual abuse, depression, and relationship concerns.

I assess and develop mentoring plans individually. How can I help you? I work one on one, in person, by telephone and other modalities can be arranged. It is all about you!

I believe, I am an expert at doing LIFE, and that I am an exceptional example who can help you and your business grow. I will stand with you because my greatest strength is perseverance. I do not give up! I fight the battle. I keep on going until I succeed. I am consistently learning who I am, how I can improve, and then I share my insight with others.

When my husband and I were approached by New York Best Selling Authors and asked to promote personal and professional leadership information, we exuberantly accepted. As leadership trainers we offer these spectacular life-changing products to interested folks. We enjoy helping others by building an income compensating community and consulting with new friends in this area.

My inspiration is expressed in my favourite mottos. "Life isn't about finding yourself. Life is about creating yourself." "Success is not the key to happiness. Happiness is the key to success." "If you love what you are doing, you will be successful."

Women Who Persevere Achieve Their Dreams – Do You Believe?

Some Books that have Influenced My Life

"Rascal" by Chris Brady - New York Best Seller
I love this book because, "Rascals are willing to step out of line and pursue their own dreams, not conform to the wishes of the masses. Rascals fear insignificance more than they fear peer pressure; they fear losing more than they fear change; they fear endless talk more than dangerous actions. I believe that everyone has inside of them a rascal, but it has been buried by endless, mind-numbing conditioning to be part of the herd."

"The Magic of Thinking Big" by David J. Schwartz, Ph.D.
More than 6 Million readers around the world

- Turn defeat into victory: there is a good side to every situation.
- Think and dream creatively: stretch your mind.
- A goal is a dream acted upon: use goals to help you grow.
- Think like a leader: you are lifted to success by those around you.

"Financial Fitness"

The Offense, Defense and Playing Field of Personal Finance by
Orrin Woodward and Chris Brady
Now in curriculum in schools and colleges

Here are encouraging quotes from two well-known individuals who are great examples of perseverance. Let us hear and live out these amazing words.

Steve Jobs was an entrepreneur, marketer and inventor who was the co-founder, chairman and CEO of Apple Inc. He stated:

"Everything around you that makes up life was made by people that are no smarter than you, you can change it, you can influence it, you can build things that other people can use."

"Here's to the crazy ones. The misfits, the rebels, the troublemakers, and the round pegs in the square holes.The ones who see things differently...they change things. They push the human race forward. And while some may see them as the crazy ones, we see them as genius."

"It (what you choose to do) has to be something that you're passionate about, otherwise, you won't have the perseverance to see it through."

Whoopi Goldberg has a fascinating life story of failure and success. Here is a snippet. She says, even as a young child she knew she was different from the rest of the world. Later, she was diagnosed with attention deficit disorder and dyslexia. She was raised in the projects in New York City.

She says, *"I am who I am and I am OK."* She is a living story of success. We all know her work. The stardom and awards she has earned are impressive. I quote, *"Appreciate success in all its forms."* What a message to women!

Reflections

1.
I believe - Women Who Persevere Achieve Their DREAMS! — DO YOU?
Owning a business can be discouraging sometimes. Several comments that I have experienced are, "I will watch you to see if you succeed" and "you don't have what it takes to make it in your own business" or "just get a 'real' job." All I can say is when the opposition comes, I am like a bull who charges, my head down and horns straight ahead. I get stronger, not weaker, because I am determined to succeed. Hold Onto Your Dream!

2.
Are You a Rascal? Do you want to be a Rascal?
A Rascal is a person who changes a negative into a positive and will not allow negativity to overtake them. A strong and going forward individual.

3.
How can I overcome my insecurities to become a secure, confident woman?
I have learned from others. Why re-work the wheel when it is already in place and working well. Hold your head up high and learn about "Rasculinity."

4.
Why is personal growth important for the growing of your business?
Your business is you. You must know your purpose.

5.
Why is financial fitness a necessity in life?
Learn the Offense, Defense and Playing Field of Personal Finance. Financial principles bring freedom.

6.
How do you handle stress and pressure? Work-life balance, understanding and implementing in your life is a necessity. Plan, Do, Check and Adjust are principals that save lives and businesses.

MENTORING
WOMEN LEADERS

Lil Lezarre

Lil Lezarre, transformation guide, entrepreneur, co-author of eight bestsellers, and professional speaker, knows what it takes to have success on the inside. This is what she's been able to accomplish with the help of mentors and coaches: She started a bra shop from scratch and building it into a fulltime business and currently working on making 'Tender Loving Cups' a franchise opportunity. Lil invented her own guiding service to help people rediscover themselves and build themselves up from the inside and offers very unique retreats that focus on you and include a day of climbing in the mountains and last, but not least, the opportunity to be in this book.

ONCE A PROTEGE.... NOW A MENTOR

Lil Lezarre

Coaches and mentors will help you on your journey, from helping you gain clarity to figuring out where you want to go. We are capable of so much and life is fun when you're living your passion. It's also a lot of work and here's the first step:

INVEST IN YOURSELF: It wasn't until I became an entrepreneur that I had no guilt about investing in myself. Only then did I start to see personal health and wellness as a business expense and now that I'm living the results of my investments, I also realize the importance of it and how big the payoff is. There's always somewhere to grow. I'm not talking about a stressful, push you to your limits kind of way. I'm talking about having a dream or a vision and pursuing it. It's amazing what surrounding yourself with great mentors and coaches can do to help you gain the skills that boost your self-confidence and transform your life.

To begin, examine yourself and explore your interests (research and development). What do you enjoy doing? What takes you to that 'world of no cares'? It makes life so much more enjoyable on a whole different, deeper, soul level. In business, as in so much of life, when pursuing your passions, you will have the drive to do it and do it well. It will take you to another world.

Time is a valuable investment that too often gets overlooked. In order to really feel good about yourself you have to build yourself up from the inside. Society has taught us to feel guilty about treating ourselves well; "they" tell us we're being selfish. Guess what, that's wrong. The more you build yourself on the inside — the more you have to give. This is all about you, what puts that smile on your face when you look in the mirror? If it's nice nails, get that manicure or pedicure. Invest some time into yourself.

Only you know what makes you excited inside. For me, my recreation time is our Canadian Rockies and because of me pursing my passions of rock and ice climbing, I am now able to add a very unique experience for my guiding packages — a day of climbing in the mountains. Believe me, my kids benefit big time from having a mom who is happy and content. I'm always there for them and here's the biggie — I'm in response mode instead of reaction mode when things happen. Ever find yourself getting so mad that things are coming out of your mouth and as they're coming out you're thinking — I don't want to say this, but it keeps coming — that's reaction mode. Your lips are moving and you can't stop them. There's actually a physical reason that's happening and I'll explain later when talking about meditation. Response is when you can think about what you're going to say. Take your time to ask questions and make the other person think for themselves, you're simply guiding them to come up with their own solution to the problem and grow from the experience. One of the steps to getting to this point is doing things that you love to do; it gives you a contented feeling on the inside and things that are out of your control don't bug you as much. It really does make a huge difference on your reactions, in all areas of your life.

Surround yourself with positive and supportive people. Networking is a must for businesses to get your name out there, but you also get so much inspiration when you see how others are succeeding and they are willing to share their expertise with you. I call that the 'positive circle' and you rise higher at every event you attend. Keep trying different organizations till you find the ones that work for you. You should walk out of every meeting with a new piece of knowledge and connected with someone new. Remove all toxic people from your life; they hold you back from succeeding. They have a way of "guilting" you and you will never grow as long as they have control over you. Supportive people encourage you to do what's right for you, they are excited for your successes instead of being jealous, they help you soar, they believe in you.

You will know when you've found the right mentor or coach, they click with you. Not everyone will and don't stop looking till you find the right one and you will soar.

Here's a list of just a few of my mentors and coaches:

One of my earliest business investments was attending a networking group for female entrepreneurs, Womanition, founded by Dorothy Briggs. This woman is all about networking and she exudes the love for what she does and supports you in every way she can. I was a Protégé in the first mentorship program Dorothy offered in 2014. My mentor, Bonnie Powers, showed me how valuable my time was, the most valuable commodity. I have the honour of being a mentor in the 2016 program. That's what happens when you invest in yourself — you grow and doors of opportunity are continually opening in front of you.

Kate Gardner, my life coach, has helped me peel back so many layers. She opened my eyes to see my limiting beliefs and negative self-talk. You have to become aware of it before you can plow through the roadblocks it places in front of you. I now help others to see their limiting beliefs and negative self-talk — that's part of the positive circle.

I hired image consultant Shirley Borrelli. I attend a lot of luncheons and wanted to have a professional look. She pointed out my hour-glass figure and told me I should be showing it off. She asked me 'what was I trying to hide' by wearing clothes with extra long sleeves and a couple sizes too large. She helped me peel back another layer on the wall I had built up — a good coach does that. I never expected to see a new Lil Lezarre that I actually like looking at in the mirror. Now I am constantly getting compliments about my knock-out outfits and tiny waist. A huge self-confidence booster.

Yvonne Racine helped me to see what my true values were, and how by not living by them, I was heading down the road to self-destruction. She also showed me the importance of treating myself with empathy and compassion, just as I do to others. Now I forgive myself when I make a mistake, learn from it and grow. Life is definitely more enjoyable when you're not beating yourself up.

Karen Trautman Sievwright, a nutrition and wellness specialist, explained to me in a way that resonated with me the importance of a healthy, well balanced diet and I actually followed her advice. I always knew I should eat right, but never did anything about it. She was very adamant that I start eating breakfast every day, but she also showed me baby steps to start eating healthier. At first I lost weight, it freaked me out because I wasn't trying to and I thought there was something wrong. Karen explained my body was going into starvation mode because I wasn't eating breakfast, now it's releasing the excess. Now I am feeling great, actually enjoying the taste and textures of fruit and vegetables (never liked them before) and realize the importance of eating a healthy, well-balanced diet.

I wanted to add some humour to my public speaking presentations and experienced a different kind of coaching with the humorous Zandra Bell. Not only did she help me with my elevator speech, she also came up with my 'Uplift' title. She's more than a coach, Zandra has become a collaborator and friend.

The latest tool I've added to my toolbox is meditation and thanks to Mandy Trapp I can now share my passion for this tool with others as a Certified Teacher. I tried different organizations for years, but couldn't meditate. Finally, Mandy taught exactly what I needed. 'Do what's right for me, whether it's laying or sitting, either is OK'. Meditation is amazing, the health benefits are endless and it's free. Meditation relaxes the mind. The Amygdale is the part of our brain that decides if something is a threat and sends our body into fight or flight mode and the Amygdale perceives 'stress' as a threat. When it's engaged, it cuts off circuitry to our prefrontal cortex (the logical thinking part of our brain). It is physically impossible to think straight or rational when the Amygdale is engaged. It's busy getting our body ready for fight or flight and we are now facing so many health issues from our bodies living in this fight or flight mode. One of the effects is going into reaction mode. Meditation is easy, all you have to do is find the right process that works for you and you will be able to do it. It's all about totally relaxing and it is life changing. I'm definitely more relaxed, sleep better, and live in response mode.

The last person I have to mention, although, not just a mentor, also one of my best friends, Donna McColl. She helps me with all my marketing, edits all my work (probably really weird for her to be editing this paragraph), and just a fun person to hang out with. She has taught me so much about writing, 'what's in it for the reader?' We actually met on an ice climbing trip and I can't count the number of ice/rock climbing and skiing trips we've done together. Our work retreats are the best. We are so productive after a day in the mountains doing what we love to do, inspiration and clarity run at the highest levels.

We all know how important it is for a business to always be putting money back into itself in order for it to grow, it's part of the budget. What's wrong with you being important enough to yourself, to invest in yourself to help you grow?

I now live my life on my terms, doing what's best for me and don't feel guilty about investing in myself. I am fulfilled on the inside and it's so rewarding to share my experiences with others and help them fulfill themselves. We will always need mentors and coaches because, as humans, we are always growing. I am so excited that I've come from being a Protégé, to now being a Mentor.

My 'self' business has grown so much from my investments. When I look in the mirror, I am proud of who I see and love who's looking back at me.

Reflections

Ready to start your self-discovery journey:

1.
When was the last time you did something for yourself? This is about you, not what others are telling you you'd enjoy. What makes you tingle inside at the very thought of doing it?

2.
When was the last time you tried something new? What is something that you've always wanted to try but were either scared or thought it was silly?

3.
When are you going to schedule both of the above answers?

Invest In Yourself. Your return on investment is immeasurable – it's that great.

Your 'Uplift Expert' and Transformation Guide

PTDS Program - Post Traumatic Divorce Self
I wrote this program for the parent who is trying to do the right thing, will not give up their values of honesty, does not bullshit and tired of getting dealt it. You feel like you're getting the short end of the stick around every corner. I've been there and I know what it takes to survive and move on and I show you with baby steps.

Meditation Teacher
Have you tried meditation but you weren't able to relax? There is a process to relaxing your mind and body. Join me at my 'Intro to Meditation' class to understand that process.

Unique Retreats
Looking for a retreat that brings you a whole new awareness about yourself, then you do something you've never done before – 1 day of climbing in our majestic Canadian Rockies. Lil has been climbing for almost a decade and where better to show you how to enjoy life to the fullest.

Public Speaker
Lil delivers uplifting life lessons in a way that is heartfelt, powerful and memorable. Attendees gain insight and practical information into numerous aspects of improving personal and professional relationships, keeping the lines of communications open within families and surviving a traumatic divorce.

Lil Lezarre

Pam McCormack

Pam McCormack owner of Body & Soul Day Spa has achieved recognition in the beauty Industry, at National and International level.

She is a Master Esthetician, Reflexologist, Reiki Master practitioner, Laser Technician.

Her entrepreneurial passion for the beauty industry has inspired her to seek recognition for the industry as a whole. Pam is a member of (SIAC) Spa Industry Association of Canada and Leading Spas of Canada.

She is an active member on (LSC) Standard and Practices board of directors.

Her Spa is winner of the Strathcona County and District 2012 Business of the year award.

Wings to Fly

Pam McCormack

I want to tell you a little bit about myself and where my business mentoring began. I did not know it at the time, my parents were the biggest mentors in my life. I am the second eldest of eight children and, although in the early years growing up in Ireland, we didn't have much of the finer things in life, we had one another and lots of love. My parents taught me the meaning of respect for others. My mother would say to us, "Hard work never killed anyone," but there were times after working hard at harvest time, or bringing home turf from the bog, that I thought "hard work must have killed someone." Mentoring children is very important and it starts in the home at a very early age. You reap what you sow.

In 1989, when I immigrated to Canada from Ireland, I lived in Fort McMurray for four years, then moved to Sherwood Park in 1993. My husband, Oliver, and I have lived in Sherwood Park for twenty two years; our son and daughter are both married and live in Sherwood Park and Ardrossan. We are proud grandparents of six beautiful grandchildren, who are our pride and joy.

After the birth of my daughter in 1981, I experienced a lot of back pain and went to see a Reflexologist. I was so in awe of the results that I wanted to know everything about it. I took my reflexology and my Reiki Master Practitioner certification and so began my curiosity for the beauty industry. I attended the Alberta Academy of Esthetics, passing with honours, but then had to decide what direction to take in my profession. I worked at a spa for three years after I finished school, but I found myself at loose ends – being older, I knew I wanted to follow my dream. It was now or never. I would have to take drastic measures and leave the security of my job to pursue the reality of owning my own business. "Better to have tried and failed, than not to have tried at all."

Moving to Alberta gave me the opportunity to accomplish my dream. They say everything comes at a price and mine was leaving family and friends in Ireland, having to overcome heartache and homesickness. There were times I considered moving back to Ireland. I really suffered from the guilt of not being there when my husband's parents passed away. My father had a triple bypass in 2003. These were the toughest days of my life, and I am happy to say he celebrated his eighty second birthday this year. My mom has had two knee replacement operations – I just don't know where she gets her energy. I guess you can't keep a good woman down.

In 2002, Body & Soul Day Spa became a reality, leasing a building with 1,500 square feet and ten employees. In 2006, we expanded the business to 3,000 square feet, bringing the staff to twenty. In 2011, we purchased a 5,900 square foot building and moved to a new location 2012. The extra space gave us the opportunity to introduce a Hair Studio as it was time for a new venture. The move was an experience I will never forget. I employed thirty staff and, like myself, we all had bills to pay, so the move was done without missing a beat. Body & Soul Day Spa closed at the old location and opened in the new location in two days. It was physically and mentally stressful, but after about six months or so the new location started to feel like home. I had loyal staff, family, and friends who worked around the clock to make this transition happen.

Meeting Dorothy Briggs and being a part of Womanition gave me the opportunity to meet other amazing women in business. I was out grocery shopping and I picked up Dorothy's first magazine. I really liked what I saw and I wanted to be part of this magazine. I phoned Dorothy that day and became part of Womanition. I am still a part of this magazine today. I admire Dorothy's business sense and sense of humour.

The metamorphosis of Body & Soul Day Spa happened in 2012 when we won the Strathcona County Chamber of Commerce Business of the Year Award. What a great feeling to hear your name called. It was the icing on the cake, so to speak. I felt all the hard work had paid off. I dedicated my award to my parents who could not be there on the night, but who were proud of my success. On the same night, we also were nominated for the Comfort Zone Long Time Service award in Rome, Italy.

I am always thinking how I can make the spa industry better and I had been searching for an entity for Esthetics. It was at a trade fair in Vancouver when I first heard of Leading Spas of Canada. It was suggested by a business acquaintance that this association might be the entity I was looking for, for our business. Joining SIAC (Spa Industry Association of Canada) and Leading Spas of Canada has given the business a voice and, in 2013, I was asked by Leading Spas of Canada to be on the Standard and Practices board of directors. Since joining, I have learned where this dedicated group are going with the industry, and I want to be part of that journey.

Leading Spa of Canada Quality Assurance Program is the only national program of its kind in the Canadian spa industry, and is designed to demonstrate to consumers which spas exceed industry standard and best practices. Spas earn the distinctive Quality Assurance Approved designation through an assessment conducted by independent third-party assessors specially trained for this industry. Renewal is not automatic and spas must re-qualify once their terms expire. Body & Soul Day Spa is the only Quality Assurance Approved Spa in Sherwood Park.

Where do I want to see the Spa Industry going over the next ten years? I know that I will work very hard to improve spa Standards and Practices. I would like to see continuing education in the esthetic industry that gives estheticians the recognition they deserve. The spa industry is ever changing and I intend on changing with it to help steer it in the right direction.

Outside of the spa business, my passion is in local theatre and performing arts. I have directed and preformed in many stage productions over the years. It is very important to have a balance in your life and theatre is mine. I love acting, singing, and dancing – it's good for the body and soul. It was my father who mentored this part of my life, putting me on a stage at twelve years old. My father has a great passion for the arts and can recite poetry, tell stories, and sing songs. When we were children we would go to visit our Nana on Sunday while our mother prepared dinner. Dad would pile all us kids into the back of the car and we wouldn't be five minutes down the road before he would have us all singing at the top of our voices. This is one of the great memories of my childhood. In 2014, my parents celebrated their 60th wedding anniversary and my two brothers and five sisters sang, "I have a life that's good" to a standing ovation. It was a moment I will cherish forever.

Starting a theatre group is great fun and lots of work. You surround yourself with people who are positive, funny, and caring. Our little group, which we named "Into the Light Productions," is a group of women who get together and put on shows and donate the proceeds to charity. This makes it so worthwhile. As a group of women, we had to find a show that would suit us all so we decided on Nunsense shows by Dan Goggins. We have donated the proceeds to groups such as Wings of Providence, Operation Smile, Make a Wish Foundation, etc. Even though I directed and acted in these shows it was team effort that made them a success.

I would like to share this reflection poem with you. I read it to remind myself to take time for the things in life that really matter to me – it is not mine, but the author is unknown.

Life's Journey (Untitled)

> Do not undermine your worth by comparing yourself with others
> It is because we are different that each of us is special
> Do not set your goals by what other people deem important
> Only you know what is best for you.
> Do not take for granted the things closest to your heart
> Cling to them as you would your life, for without them life is meaningless
> Do not let your life slip through your fingers by living in the past nor the future
> By living your life one day at a time, you live all the days of your life
> Do not give up when you still have something to give
> Nothing is really over until the moment you stop trying
> It is a fragile thread that binds us to each other
> Do not be afraid to encounter risks.
> It is by taking chances that we learn how to be brave
> Do not shut love out of your life by saying it is impossible to find.
> The quickest way to receive love is to give love
> The fastest way to lose love is to hold it too tightly
> In addition, the best way to keep love is to give it wings
> Do not dismiss your dreams
> To be without dreams is to be without hope
> To be without hope is to be without purpose.
> Do not run through life so fast that you forget not only where you have been, but where you are going
> Life is not a race, but a journey to be savored each step of the way.

I hope you enjoyed hearing a little bit about my experiences in business and in life. It is an honour for me to be part of this book with so many other successful business women. I wish them all every success in their future endeavours. To be successful in business you have to have your heart in your business and your business in your heart. When you think about it, most successful business people were people who had an idea and made it a reality by believing in themselves.

To my parents, thank you so much for being my mentors. Even though it was hard to leave you, you gave me wings to fly, to be successful, and to call Sherwood Park home.

It goes without saying that the success of our business is because of our dedicated clientele, without whom, our business would not exist. I thank you all from the bottom of my heart for being part of the journey that has made us the successful business we are today.

Reflections

1.

What in my story did you find mentoring to you personally?

We all mentor in one way or another. For me it started with my parents, which in turn gave me the values I had to mentor my children. I feel the biggest mistake parents make is doing too much for their children. The only way to be successful is to learn from your mistakes

2.

Do you have support in your life from someone, be it family or friends?

I have had lots of support over the years from family and friends, but the backbone of the business is my husband, Oliver. He is the one who makes the spa run smoothly, he is the person who fixes everything from plumbing to electrical. He is always there to listen, he is my rock.

3.

From an emigrant's point of view what was the most difficult change you had to make when you came to Canada?

When I look back, the biggest hurdle I had was climate. That first winter in Ft. McMurray I almost went back to Ireland. Even though English is my first language, there were certain words I had to change. After 26 years, I still find it difficult with some of these words. People need to remember that just because you speak with an accent doesn't mean that you think with an accent.

4.

Did you ever have someone unethically try to take away everything you have worked for?

If I need new employees I put an advertisement on social media, that way if an employee from another business has decided to leave their current employment it is their decision. I don't believe it is ethical to solicit employees from other businesses by offering outrageous wage or commissions. I remember an old Irish saying, "Hills are green far away." I will never allow anyone to piggyback my business.

5.

If you were not in your current profession what who you want to do?

I don't even have to think about this one — it has to be theatre. There is no business like show business, as they say. Especially when you put so much energy into a show. It's a wonderful feeling to do it for the good of a charity.

MENTORING
WOMEN LEADERS

Sam Rafoss

Sam Rafoss is a Business Strategist for Nutrition and Holistic Practices. As a healer and a marketer, she has made it her mission to share her unique combination of spiritual and holistic business & marketing expertise to help the healers of the world attract their ideal clients and make money doing what they love to do. Sam is a member of CAPS (Canadian Association of Professional Speakers) Calgary, and is the co-author of two bestselling books. Sam is also a Certified Holistic Nutritionist™ and is the nutrition educator for the Healthy Living School Program at VIVO for the Calgary Board of Education.

4 Habits That Can Change Your Life

Sandra (Sam) Rafoss

For most of my life I have studied personal development, spiritual development and metaphysics, the branch of philosophy that examines the nature of reality. I came by it honestly from my parents. When I was growing up they read self-help books, listened to inspirational music and motivational tapes daily. I'm grateful they showed me the value of personal growth to develop self-confidence and success.

From all of my years of study and practice, there are four habits that I believe are life-changing. If you even choose one of these and make it a daily habit, it can have the power to change how you think, feel, and act.

My first habit happens to be my favourite, meditation.

Meditation

Meditation is one of the most powerful tools to tune into what your soul is yearning for. Deep. I know. And I also know what you're thinking, "I'm don't meditate", "I can't sit still", "I can't turn off my thoughts", "I won't do it right."

It was like that for me at the beginning, too. I thought I had to listen to certain music, sit a certain way, and feel a certain way. I bought CDs with guided meditation and, at time, I fell asleep! Then I chastised myself for not doing it properly and would stop doing it because it didn't seem to "work". And I wasn't even really sure what was supposed to happen. This approach went on and off for years — I'd "mediate" two or three times a week for a few months and write in one of my journals and then I'd stop for six months or more. Life would get "busy" and I thought I didn't have time to meditate. After awhile, I would start to miss the quiet time of meditation and the "messages" that often came through to me during the quiet time of introspection so I would start all over again. As I began to meditate more often, I knew I felt better. I couldn't quite pinpoint what it was, I just knew I felt more at peace and balanced in my life.

I don't make New Year's Resolutions, but I do make one promise to myself at the beginning of every year. Sometimes I make more than one, but I've made an agreement with my higher self, that as long as I keep one yearly promise, that's personal growth.

January 1, 2014 the promise was "to meditate, pray, and journal daily if even for 2 minutes, I would commit to do it before anything else." As I declared that promise to myself and the Universe, I felt the shift within my heart and soul and I knew I would keep the promise.

Meditation is like exercise. The more you do it, the more your body craves and needs it. I feel "off" if I don't meditate first thing in the morning. Some mornings, it may be a 2 minute silence and prayer for a blessed day and other mornings I leisurely meditate, pray, and journal for over an hour.

I noticed after about six months of consistency that reoccurring messages kept showing up. I felt more confident in my personal and business decisions. When you mediate daily, you really tune into your intuition and can make sound decisions quickly. Let's face it, in our fast-paced world, this is a bonus to learn to trust our intuition even when it doesn't make logical sense.

I encourage you to try meditation. Try your "own" way. It can be just learning to sit in silence and listen to your own thoughts. If that doesn't feel right to you and you need more structure, you may want to try a guided meditation. There are lots of different ones on You Tube.

The next habit is Appreciation.

Appreciation

It is so easy to identify what's not working in our lives and dwell on it. We all go through disappointment and heartache. After my divorce a few years ago, I was at a very low point. I worried about my children, my business, and my finances. It was tough to shake out of my own pity party, but I knew I had to if I was going to feel better personally and reach my business goals.

I remembered reading in one of the Law of Attraction books, Abraham-Hicks talking about "flooding your own vibrational patterns of thought with appreciation." So that is exactly what I did. I began to focus on gratitude and appreciation for my family, my clients, my friends, my health, my finances. No matter what was happening, I chose to look for the silver-lining and there is always one if you look.

I'm not saying it's easy. It takes a concerted effort to be aware of your thoughts and keep them positive, but I was determined to keep at it. Thoughts truly do drive what happens in your life. I soon realized whatever you appreciate, appreciates. Whatever you focus on expands is a fundamental principle of the Law of Attraction.

One of my favourite spiritual intuitives is Colette Baron-Reid. I printed and framed a quote of hers to hang on my wall where I read it throughout the day – "What you are is what you attract."

A powerful statement that reminds me, what I want to receive is what I have to give.

If I want happiness, I have to be happy. If I want health, I have to be healthy. You get it.

So, I encourage you to appreciate and give thanks for everything in your life. Even the struggles and disappointments, give thanks, for they truly do make us stronger and lead us to the good.

Take a moment and reflect on the times in your life where the "darkness" led you to the "light" and give thanks and celebrate.

The third habit is good communication skills.

Communication

For good communication it is important to be honest with yourself and others. Have the courage to say what you really want. Never assume people can read your mind. Listen to your intuition and do what is best for you first. What I mean by this, is take care of your needs in order to be healthy and happy and you will be able to do the same for others. It is impossible to please all of the people in your life all of the time but some people do try hard to do just that.

Often women put themselves and their needs last. I used to say "yes" to everything early on in my entrepreneurial journey and it is what I see from many of my clients.

Women so often "over give" or worry about other people's needs first. This comes from a place of good intention that usually results in the opposite.

I'm sure you can think of many times you have said "yes" when you wish you would have said "no". There is a balance between giving and receiving. When you "over give", you get out of balance.

If you feel like you give too much, it's time to practice saying "no". It really is okay to say "no". Often people are happy when you do. You are being honest with yourself and them. When you say "yes" and only can give a part of yourself, you are not really helping when you have stretched yourself too thin. It is a disservice to both parties.

The same goes for asking for what you want. Have the courage to ask for what you want.

You will never get what you want if you don't decide what you want and communicate clearly with confidence and believe that you deserve it. Whatever it is you want in life. You need to decide for yourself. Ask for help if you need it. There are many people who would gladly help you reach your goals, but you need to ask for what you want. Don't let fear hold you back from saying no or yes. I mean saying "yes" to investing in yourself and your business. Many women refuse to invest in themselves for fear of losing money or making a mistake.

Every successful entrepreneur I know, including myself, has had some bad experiences and lost some money along the way. It is part of the journey. Do not dwell on it. Learn from it and move on.

Look for what you can celebrate, the fourth habit.

Celebration

I used to be one of those people that only celebrated big goals. But did you know that your mind doesn't know the difference between a big goal and a little goal? It's like the "fight or flight" stress response in our body. I'm sure you've heard of it — it's our body's physiological reaction that occurs in response to a real or perceived threat. Basically, if our mind sounds the alarm, our body reacts whether we really do have to run away from a big bear chasing us or not. (It could be we are "stressed" because we are running late for work).

Well, it's the same with success. Our mind does not know the difference between achieving a big goal or a little goal. But, here's the magic. If you start to celebrate daily, every small step forward, every mini goal that brings you closer to your bigger goal, your successes multiply.

Just like what you appreciate, appreciates. When you focus on successes, it has you attract even more success. I know this because I've tried it and it works.

When I made the decision to continue my part-time business after my divorce, I was stressed about not getting clients fast enough. I started to worry about finances and the snowball started rolling. Once again, I knew from studying metaphysics that I had to change what I was focusing on in order to get a different result. I started thinking about all of the things I had accomplished and realized that I truly had achieved many small goals I hadn't even acknowledged.

Once I reminded myself of this I got back on track. I started writing down small goals and checking them off each day and celebrating and giving thanks every night before I went to sleep. This practice helped me to focus on all of the good in my life and what's working. I soon realized whatever I went to "sleep on" brought more of it. Most of the time, life is good and I go to sleep on good thoughts. Occasionally, doubt and stress creeps in and I go to bed on a worrisome thought. Guess what?

My sleep is not as good and I awake feeling anxious and "out of sorts". This is not a good feeling. The good thing is I know how to fix it quickly. I do know that sometimes my choices may be limited, but my thoughts are unlimited. I have complete control over how I think. When I choose positive thoughts and choose to celebrate the good, even in the midst of a seemingly bad situation or event, I get back what I focus on.

Acknowledge every success, no matter how small. Try keeping a daily log of all of your accomplishments. Give yourself a pat on the back and celebrate a little every day and see what happens.

These are my four daily habits for success: meditation, appreciation, communication, and celebration.mWhen you make even one of them a habit, it truly can be life-changing.

Choose one of the following and commit to do it for 30 days in a row. If you skip one day, start at Day 1 again. The key is consistency to form a new habit.

Reflections

1.
Meditation. If you are new to meditation, start with sitting in silence for 5 minutes daily at the same time. Schedule it for as soon as you wake or just before you go to bed. Set a timer if that helps.
2.
Appreciation: List who and/or what you appreciate and are thankful for. (Friends, Family, Job, Clients, Money, Health,).
3.
Communication: Practice "asking" for what you want. Start small if this is new to you. (i.e. ask a store clerk for help). By the end of 30 days your goal is to be ready for a "big ask", something you have been dreaming about but have been letting fear stop you.
4.
Celebration: Start a Celebration Log to record everything you have accomplished. If you do 30 days in a row, give yourself a bigger reward (i.e. $100 to shop, Round of Golf, Night out for dinner/movie, Spa Day).

Make a commitment to yourself by writing the following sentence in your journal or calendar:

Today, (date)_______________________________ I _____________________________ __________ commit to _____________________________ for 30 days in a row. If I skip a day, I will start at Day 1 again.

Example: Today, June 23/15, I Jane Smith commit to ask for help or for new business (i.e. pass the salt, please give me directions, call a new prospect,) for 30 days in a row. If I skip a day, I will start at Day 1 again.
(Sign it)
At the end of 30 days, list your thoughts on the exercise you chose. Write freely or use some of these writing prompts.
I feel...
I thought I would feel...
I learned...
I will continue with...
I am proud of myself because...

Bonus Offer from Sam Rafoss

The Four Fundamentals to a Booming Holistic Business ($27 Value)

www.samrafoss.com

Bonus Offer Number Two

Check yes and then contact me for your free strategy call.

Yes! ☐ I am a healer and would love to learn how to boom my business.

Yes! ☐ I have purchased a copy of Mentoring Women Leaders.

Email sam@samrafoss.com or call toll free 1.855.860.6777 and I will schedule a 60 minute strategy call ($500 Value) with you to discuss how I can help you gain confidence, attract your ideal clients and make more money doing what you love to do.

Contact me today!

MENTORING
WOMEN LEADERS

Sandra Fisher

Sandy Fisher leads from the heart and success has no choice but to follow.
This smart and savvy mortgage expert, broker owner of Verico iMortgage Solutions, and mentor to a team of more than a score of successful mortgage specialists, will readily admit she "just loves people", undoubtedly the key to her longevity in such a challenging industry along with her enviable work ethic and "never give up" perseverance.

Of course, it doesn't hurt she typically saves her clients thousands in interest!

Her pride and joy, ten year old daughter, Ashley, is certainly her own personal inspiration, but Sandy will never tire of that special thrill she experiences repeating her magical mantra, "Guess what! YOU'VE BEEN APPROVED!!!"

Comfort Zones – Quicksand To The Soul

Sandy Fisher

"Our lives are not determined by what happens to us but by how we react to what happens..."

These may be another's words but they certainly sum up the life lessons I, myself, have learned, thanks to a very negative experience with an even more negative supervisor. This served as the catalyst for the young, timid, self effacing Sandy Fisher, a nervous, "never speak out of turn" kind of girl, to ultimately become the owner of a premiere mortgage brokerage, mentor to scores of brilliant, talented agents, now a strong, confident woman, unafraid to make the tough decisions, a proud business leader who looks forward to the future with an open minded, enthusiastic attitude that says "Bring it on…NOW!"

Believe me, this transformation definitely did not happen overnight! In fact, as a child, I always had dreams of becoming a teacher. Possessing an innate curiosity, I liked the idea of helping others reach their potential as I hoped to fulfill mine. Starting out as a bank teller instead, was a far cry from my original career aspirations, that idyllic picture in my imagination of what I wanted to be "when I grow up".

In addition, I found it discouraging that it was so difficult to move ahead if you weren't the "favourite", some nepotist's relative, or the office keener eager to ingratiate themselves babysitting the boss' kids. Undaunted though, I put my naturally inquisitive mind to work, continually asking questions of the more experienced staff willing to share ideas and expertise.

At the time I was quite disillusioned by the unprofessional behaviour and abysmal work ethic exhibited by some of the so called "managers", but now, with the wisdom of maturity enhancing my perspective, I realize they were really role models, negative ones, yes, but there, nonetheless, to demonstrate exactly what I did not want for myself. Conversely, I developed a different personal philosophy, "Work hard. Do what's right. Treat others the way you would want to be treated yourself."

Even in the business realm, my advice to novice mortgage agents would always be to focus on your client, listen to their story so you can empathize, identify their needs, and effectively intuit how best to fulfill them. When you concentrate on helping the people as opposed to counting the money, your customer base develops naturally. Building relationships is so important. Why would people choose you as their mortgage specialist? They like you. They trust in you, because you've made them feel confident in your ability to help them. I know, from experience, that perseverance and determination always pay off!

After fifteen years in banking, I found my passion, excelling as a mortgage specialist, reveling in the exhilarating high speed, high pressure "do or you're deadline" role of coordinating. Cajoling appraisers, realtors, lawyers, and lenders all for the purpose of achieving that one hugely rewarding objective, helping people finance one of the most important, deeply emotional transactions of their lives, the purchase of their home.

Most people really don't understand the mortgage broker's role. I'll admit, at one time, I'd never heard of them myself! But, make no mistake; the value we bring to the table is paramount, saving homebuyers substantial amounts of money and time. In essence, it's like a mortgage match making service. As opposed to a typical financial institution, we have access to an entire array of lenders, thus we're able to help homebuyers find a mortgage no matter what their life circumstances or monetary situation. I chose this career primarily because I love people. Buying a home is such a rite of passage in life, I am honoured and exhilarated every time I have the thrill of personally guiding someone through one of the biggest decisions they will ever make, especially when I can save them thousands of dollars in interest!

Certainly, on the job, juggling all the various balls at once is a tremendous challenge, the tight timelines, the extreme emotions, the stressful sorting through all the financially feasible permutations to facilitate each individual mortgage, but I love it all! For me, there's always a profound feeling of accomplishment when the deal is completed, especially because I'm very adamant about educating my clients, including them in the decision making process, and reassuring them every step of the way.

It's that "teacher" in me again, always compelled to instill knowledge and encourage learning. In fact, once I'd developed a thorough expertise in my mortgage specialist role, I realized that my inclination then was to mentor other aspiring agents to be their best, to help them learn from my successes, and avoid my mistakes. Miraculously, an outside career opportunity came my way to do just that, manage other mortgage specialists. Me, a sales manager? Could I do it? If I dived into these uncharted waters, was I going to sink or swim?

Stepping out of my comfort zone, I made that leap of faith in my abilities, and I am still afloat today! When opportunities present themselves, we do always have the choice, to stay with the known entity, maintain the status quo, or to make a splash, to test our boundaries and take a chance. Success finds those who apply themselves. Learning from the ground up, rolling up my metaphorical sleeves and being willing, even as a supervisor, to pitch in and do the nitty gritty activities, all this was a large part of my success.

What gave me my competitive edge? It was my penchant for being organized and consistent. I adhered faithfully to a system that facilitated tracking, developing, and building business relationships. No matter the business, its stage of development, I would strongly recommend you maintain a written plan. Stay on track. Ensure your daily, weekly, monthly activities are all in alignment working towards your greater goal. It's only natural to take a wrong turn occasionally, but with structured guidelines in place to keep you focused on the big picture, it makes it a lot easier to climb back on that "road" to success.

Mentoring my people was such a joy! Understanding their situations, their struggles and strengths, it all helped me determine how best to help them succeed. The freedom wealth provides is always a positive, but it wasn't my primary motivation. Working with incredibly diligent women making a quarter of their worth tied to mundane office jobs, and being able to inspire them, encourage their independence, build their confidence to the point they were earning over six figures, that's what made me shine inside.

Yes, I had the financial rewards, the satisfaction of nurturing my team to reach higher sales goals over and over again, but I didn't have the freedom from being manipulated and betrayed by a certain supervisory element within the organization who, compelled by his own agenda, contrived to bring me down. Yes, unfortunately, I still answered to those less than stellar supervisors who had the power to make my life a living hell. Truthfully, it was not a happy experience. I went through the whole gamut of raw emotions and personal doubts. Safe and secure in my comfort zone, I wasn't thrilled at the prospect of being poked and prodded enough to leave. In retrospect, though, had this individual not forced me to the brink, made me realize that tolerating the situation was not being true to myself, I would have never made the choice that subsequently transformed me into the thriving, self-actualized entrepreneur I have become.

"Our lives are not determined by what happens to us but by how we react to what happens..." How did I choose to react? After a quarter century working for a corporation, I made the decision to open my own firm. How fortunate this negative incident made my comfort zone way too UNcomfortable! If we don't challenge ourselves when the opportunity presents itself, the universe will simply bring about circumstances that will very inconveniently do it for us. So instead of fighting, trying to prevent the inevitable change from occurring, we should embrace these hardships and upheavals, even though that seems inconceivable at the time. In reality, these dark times are the heaven sent catalysts meant to move us forward to where we're actually meant to be.

There I was, head of my own mortgage brokerage. I thought I knew everything I needed to, but oh, did I become very humble very quickly. Yes, I still had more to learn, but, truthfully, the transformation from paid employee to business owner empowered and revitalized me, leaving me with a deep sense of pride, and resilience. I had opened my firm during a downturn in the marketplace so immediately the naysayers started predicting doom, but instead of it being a bad time, it was the perfect time. I was able to study the ins and outs of running the business thanks to the slower pace.

Once again my greatest satisfaction came from building a strong team of agents, a team, this time, that was truly mine, hand picked, savvy professionals with similar attitudes and values who wanted to work with one another, not against. I've found the best way to motivate people is to be genuine and sincere, unafraid to show you care. When you put others first, promote their best interests, your own personal rewards flow effortlessly to you, personally, professionally, and financially.

Make the change. Do it now. Had I hesitated, listened to the critics, had I not made the change, I would have been making excuses, letting my fears sabotage my progress into something new. Anytime you can challenge yourself, push yourself out of your comfort zone, you'll be amazed at how much further ahead you are at the end of the day. There is such power in making that decision to move forward.

Not so much older now, but a hell of a lot wiser, I continue on in my journey, my vocation as a mortgage broker, empowering women to really see and appreciate themselves, take the credit they deserve, so they ultimately blossom into the entrepreneurial success stories they deserve to be. Interesting how life comes full circle. In mentoring my agents, helping them learn and grow to become their personal best, my childhood dreams of becoming a teacher come true every day. I have actually grown up into what I wanted to be.

Realizing your dreams, fulfilling your true potential, it's a life long process so try not to take it all so seriously all the time. Berating yourself for your mistakes accomplishes nothing. See your setbacks not as personal failures, but as divine learning experiences instead. Have a little faith… and, a little fun! Spend time, not with those constant critics who thrive on the negative. Surround yourself instead with the people who accept and inspire you.

It's truly never too late to start living your big dream. That comfort zone may be safe, secure, but stagnant and soul destroying, as well. Don't let your fear, your disbelief in your own self-worth prevent you from taking that leap of faith into your best life. To me, you've achieved true success when you love your job so much, you wouldn't think to call it "work". When you wake up every morning looking forward to your day of being in your business, that's when you should thank your lucky stars.

Myself, I thank the unlucky setbacks in my life, too. I am grateful for every step of my way, whether they were steps forward or back. They were still part of my overall journey towards my greater goal. Those separate steps still added up to the career, the business, the life of my dreams, because, despite the adversity, I persevered, and I still kept taking them. Yes, I embraced change, and now I really love my new boss! Because, it's me.

Are you in a comfort zone, so safe, stale, and secure that it's suffocating you? So, what are you going to do?

Reflections

1.
Look back in the negative events in your life. With your current perspective what positive things actually came out of what you perceived as disastrous at the time?

2.
Are there currently negative role models in your life?

3.
What are they teaching you that is to your advantage?

4.
Are you in a comfort zone, so safe, stale, and secure that it's suffocating you?

5.
So what are you going to do?

MENTORING
WOMEN LEADERS

Shirley Borrelli

Shirley Borrelli, B.Ed. is an accomplished business strategist, award winning image consultant and C.O.N.F.I.D.E.N.C.E. coach whose services are very much sought after in entrepreneurial and corporate circles alike.

Originally trained as an educator, Shirley now effectively wields her superlative teaching talents to instruct management, sales professionals, and solopreneurs on using their outward appearance, interpersonal skills, and inner effectiveness to attract the long lasting success they desire.

An active author, magazine contributing editor, and frequent television personality, Shirley still makes time to give back to the business community through her dedicated involvement in the widely acclaimed Womanition Mentorship program.

Nothing Beats C.O.N.F.I.D.E.N.C.E.

by Shirley Borrelli, B.Ed.

Whether it's love, money or the healthy body you deserve, when it comes to getting what you want nothing beats confidence.

Confidence: it is that one all-encompassing, essential piece to your success puzzle. Confidence is the foundation of all other success strategies, such as positive thinking, visioning, meditation, time management, people skills, hard skills, goal setting, and leadership.

Studies have shown that women are 20 per cent less likely to feel competent and confident compared to their male counterparts. All things being equal, women tend to undervalue themselves as less qualified, less likely to succeed, and less likely to have what it takes to make it to the top in comparison to men.

Many books have information promising to give you the keys to success, but what they don't tell you, and what they all have in common, is that you need the C.O.N.F.I.D.E.N.C.E. to implement those strategies. Information alone is not powerful. Applied information causes changes to happen. You need the discipline, courage, and mindset to take action on those strategies. You absolutely must master the skill of believing in yourself, believing you can do it, and believing that you are worthy of the success you deserve before it will fully manifest in your life. The game of life is won first in your head and heart before it is ever won in real time.

Without enough confidence, you can be fearful that you are not cut out to succeed or that you are wasting your time, money, and energy chasing a dream that will never come true. You know you have the skills, talent, and ambition, yet somehow the long-lasting success you seek seems just out of reach. If you are struggling to believe in yourself and your dreams, you may be sabotaging your success without even being aware that your inner core beliefs are keeping you from your desired outcome.

Perhaps, you are looking to build confidence in the people around you because confident people inspire confidence in others. I'm not talking about a loud, arrogant kind of confidence that takes over the conversation in a room. Confidence is quiet. Insecurities are loud.

My passion is to help you achieve the success you desire. Why? Because at one time I wasn't as confident as I am today. Life is more fulfilling being confident than it is living afraid, insecure, and doubtful. I've since learned what it takes to break through and come out more complete, happier and more successful on the other end. Back then, I felt invisible, unaccomplished, and unworthy of success. I thought every time someone wanted to talk to me, I was somehow in trouble. I believed everybody was better than me and that I needed to please them in order to be liked.

I grew up on a farm in a small rural town. Although I had been the president of many school clubs, the captain of various sports teams, and had received academic and athletic awards, I focused strongly on pleasing others. As long as people were happy and approving of me, I must be ok…right?

I really loved playing volleyball in high school. I had won Most Valuable Player awards in both my 11th and 12th grades in high school, was the assistant captain and then moved on to being captain of the team. I had always dreamed of playing volleyball professionally one day.

When I was accepted to the University of Alberta's Faculty of Education — it was my chance to try out for the University varsity team— the Pandas. I had an opportunity to pursue one of my goals and to make one of my dreams come true.

Unfortunately, my low self-confidence and limiting inner beliefs blocked me from trying out for the team. I convinced myself that I was too short, too fat, and not skilled enough. I gave myself negative self-talk, saying big city girls make the team, not small town kids like me. I convinced myself that I wasn't good enough and shouldn't even try to make the team; I wasn't going to make it anyways.

Over time, I learned that my limiting inner core beliefs were keeping me from living life to the fullest. I was unaware that my crippled confidence was keeping me hostage in a small world. My life was reduced to only what was safe, guaranteed, and non-threatening. How could I expect to live an exciting, prosperous, and fulfilling life if I never pushed past my comfort zone and risk failure, embarrassment, and take a chance to succeed? Even to this day, I get quite emotional about the time I defeated myself before even trying. I dreamt about playing for the Pandas, but stood in my own way and bought into my fear of failure by never trying out for the team. I had to learn how to build myself up and give myself permission to be embarrassed, to try and maybe even fail. But what if I have made the team? What if I had succeeded? How might that have changed the future of my entire life? Because I lacked the confidence to even show up for the tryout, I will never know my missed opportunities.

Because of my experiences, I want to help you become the person you've always wanted to be — the person you love from the inside out and the person who naturally draws in others.

There is no long lasting joy when you are not clear on your purpose. One might think only shy, nervous, withdrawn people need a boost of confidence. Not always. Often it is the overachieving, life of the party extrovert who needs a healthy overhaul of how they feel about themselves. Over the years of building my confidence and the confidence of my clients, I learned there were many indicators of a lack of confidence. Here are 10 of the most common signs your confidence could use a boost:

1. **You overthink everything.** It is good to gather information to review and analyze so you can plot your course, but when you think things over too much, you may feel overwhelmed and confused. Doubt sets in.
2. **You procrastinate.** You are unable to make a decision and take action because you are afraid to make a mistake. However, you tell yourself it's because you are too busy to think about the issue at hand. Inactivity is keeping your life safe, but small. Like the saying goes, "A ship is safe in the harbour, but that's not what ships are built for."
3. **You defeat yourself before you even try.** You convince yourself with false evidence that a favourable outcome is not possible; therefore, you don't even begin. You avoid any kind of forward action so you can avoid failure. You convince yourself that you aren't ready, capable or qualified and that you are not good or experienced enough to achieve success. You make excuses to justify your lack of trying.
4. **You blame others, situations or circumstances for your current state of affairs.** By doing so, you freely give your power away to others. You often feel like a victim.

5. **You undermine your value.** You don't receive compliments well. You deflect them. You minimize your work, results, capabilities, potential and earning power.
6. **You are hard on yourself.** You easily cut other people slack, but you are very unforgiving to yourself. You beat yourself up with negative self-talk and you don't easily let go of disappointments.
7. **You've become a people pleaser.** This goes beyond being easy to get along with or trying to satisfy and meet people's needs because you are a team player. A people pleaser actually NEEDS others' approval in order to feel good about themselves. In extreme cases, women in abusive relationships have been conditioned to walk on eggshells to not upset their abuser. This is very damaging to one's self-esteem and self-confidence. Professional help is recommended.
8. **You are afraid to raise your prices.** You fear asking for more money or a long overdue raise or promotion. You are afraid to risk the security of what you presently have.
9. **You avoid attending events, meeting new people or trying new things.** Stretching your comfort zone requires courage. When you only live in your comfort zone, you keep yourself from experiencing new, exciting and what might be the most rewarding opportunities of your lifetime.
10. **You talk, a lot.** Deep down, nervous people feel unworthy, awkward or like they have something to prove. That is why they often dominate a conversation without doing much listening. It requires a quiet internal confidence to do more listening than talking. It is difficult to learn and expand your life when you are doing all the talking. It has been said that we all have two ears and one mouth to suggest doing twice as much listening and half as much talking. Learn how to engage others to talk. Learn how to listen and be genuinely interested in other people.

These are signs of a lack of confidence, but you can learn the skills and strategies you need to get out of your own way and get all the things you desire out of life. If you recognized yourself in any of the descriptions, it is time to give yourself a confidence boost so you can live your life more freely and completely.

I have used fashion, style, and image consulting for years as my tools to help clients understand and build their confidence. Now, my 10 module C.O.N.F.I.D.E.N.C.E. program takes a deeper dive into body language and personal skills. Most importantly, we explore your inner belief system to help you understand and build your confidence and the confidence of the people around you.

Let's start by defining confidence so you can see that it is truly the foundation of all other strategies for success. The dictionary definition says that "Confidence is a belief, a conviction that an outcome will be favourable." Another standard definition is "A certainty of something" and the third reads, "A belief in the effectiveness of one's own abilities or in one's favourable acceptance by others."

You want to attract that success to your life. My C.O.N.F.I.D.E.N.C.E. program takes each letter in the word "confidence" and dives deeper so you can implement strategies to experience a positive shift in your success.

C: Competence: Know that you can do the job.
O: Outcomes: Getting results will build your confidence.
N: No negatives: Negativity repels success from you.
F: First impressions: What are people getting from you? Is your image projecting your intended message?
I: Inner beliefs: How to believe in yourself.
D: Decisive: Get clear direction and take action.
E: Extrovert: Even an introvert can smile and learn to be more outgoing.
N: Non-verbal communication skills: Body language, facial expressions, hand gestures, how you walk and how you hold your body posture are speaking for you before you say a single word.
C: Charisma: Attract people like a magnet.
E: Excellence: Choose excellence, not perfection. There is a difference. Excellence also involves overcoming procrastination.

Maybe you have missed opportunities or your fear prevents you from making important decisions. Maybe you have fear of attending events, speaking up, talking to people, meeting new people, or looking attractive. Those fears are keeping your life small.

The world needs you to show up in a bigger way. What's stopping you? I'm guessing it is confidence in yourself and the people around you. People can hear you talk, but can they feel your presence? I'm talking about the internal self-assurance you project. That self-assurance is what attracts people to you in a very positive way. When you attract people, you can more fully share your gifts with the world.

When it comes to attracting all those good things you deserve, **Nothing Beats C.O.N.F.I.D.E.N.C.E.**

Reflections

Whether it's love, money or health, when it comes to getting what you want, nothing beats confidence! Confidence is required to take action on success principles.

1. Jot down a number from 1-10 to rate your current level of confidence. 1 is low confidence where you struggle to look at yourself in the mirror. 10 is the highest level of confidence: you never doubt yourself and you believe you can accomplish anything.

____

____

2. Write why you feel your confidence is currently at that level. Let the answers flow. Don't prejudge them, edit them or evaluate them. Write down what's coming freely to you right now.

____

____

____

____

Baselines are important to mark the starting point so that when you look back overtime, you will be able to measure your journey and make the appropriate plans going forward.

3. Jot down a number from 1-10 to rate your IDEAL level of confidence. 1 is the lowest and 10 is highest.

____

____

The difference from where your confidence is now (current) and where you want it to be (IDEAL) is called your "confidence gap". The gap can be filled by using my 10 module confidence building program available online at www.shirleyborrelli.com/nbc

4. Write down why you want your confidence to be at this IDEAL level? What will your life look like at this level? Be as specific as possible. If you are able, find pictures to be a visual representation of your ideal confident life. Paste those pictures on a vision board to remind yourself daily of where you are headed in the future because of who you are becoming as a person.

____
____
____
____

5. Why are the answers in #4 important to you? Be honest with yourself. Often these are the painful things in your life you want to move away from.

____
____
____
____
____
____

6. In order to have a shift in your confidence to attract more success to your life, you need strategies. You need a plan. These strategies then need to be implemented into your daily life. You probably already know what needs to change in order to grow your confidence. If not, stand in front of a mirror. Look at the person you see. Ask her "what do I need to do to grow my confidence?" Write down what she told you:

____
____
____
____

If you are unclear how to grow your confidence or if you know you need some expert advice how to make a plan and create strategies to be more confident, call Shirley for your FREE Confidence Boost coaching call. 780.235.5506.

MENTORING
WOMEN LEADERS

What the Protégés are Saying...

I decided to invest in the Womanition mentorship group without really knowing what I was getting myself into. I'd seen an advertisement in the back of Womanition magazine, and I knew I needed to do something to get my business going, because I didn't want to go back to getting a "real" job. I decided to take the plunge.

Every effort was to make me feel welcome and comfortable from the start. The meetings are always informative and it has been great meeting other women in the same boat as I am in. My own mentor has been very generous with her time and expertise and I'm grateful to have been able to draw on the expertise of some of the other mentors who have been equally generous.

I would recommend this program to anyone considering starting a business or trying to take their business to the next level. These women are phenomenal!

Cindy Koistinen

I have learned many things so far from my mentor such as: developing a streamlined system for my own business as well as others; client evaluation to figure out the right type of clients for my business profile; changing my LinkedIn profile to look more professional rather than be a resume format; SWOT analysis overview to ensure I was on the right track; taking personal breaks for myself, spouse, and pets; review my hourly cost to make sure it's in line with others in the same type of business. I think this Mentorship program is a great opportunity to engage with the mentors of various backgrounds to find out if there is anything that can assist with my business' growth and potentially develop new ideas from the experiences of the mentors whether it be their personal and/or professional success.

Bonnie Jensen Walker

A little over a year ago I enrolled in the Womanition Mentorship program. I wasn't sure what I was looking for from the program, but I knew that something I desperately needed was a mentor to help me take my business to the next level. I was happily matched up with the perfect mentor for my current businesses state. This person sat with me and said, how can I help you in your business? It was like someone lifted a huge weight off of my shoulders; I felt safe, validated and, encouraged. I was able to open up about the realities and questions I was facing with my business. I was given solid advice and real time solutions. I felt motivated and confident and that began to show in the clients I attracted. Every month we would meet as a group and I would have access to the other mentors in the program. This further spurred me forward as I soaked up, like a sponge, the knowledge they shared.

Since then, I have seen my sales more than double, I have a clear sense of direction, my client base has grown, and I love the feeling of confidence I have in what I am doing and how I am doing it. I know that a huge part of my success was being a part of the Womanition Mentorship Program!

Candice Smiley

The mentorship program has been an amazing experience. I have been able to learn from 13 mentors who are experts in many different fields. This program is unbelievably priced. Nowhere else you could have a once a month connection with 26 amazing woman and have private one on one sessions with your own mentor over a 6 month period for this price. This program keeps me accountable and committed to what I want.

Lisa Goodwin

I have found my experience in the mentorship program to be very helpful with my perspective on my business. My Mentor was absolutely amazing. She has shifted my way of thinking enough so that people have noticed a positive change. I have gone out of my comfort zone professionally and personally. I will be interested in doing the program again as there is so much to learn from the amazing Mentors in this program.

Victoria Armstrong

To have a vision of what you want to accomplish is the first step. To see a clear path to your end result is something else. How do you do it? You don't know what you don't know! Being a protégé in the Womanition Mentorship Program has helped to guide me on the journey to my success. They know, what I don't know, and I am very fortunate to be able to learn from them all.

Debra Couwenberg

I was a protégé in the first mentorship program and it was an incredible experience. The wealth of knowledge shared among the mentors and protégé was extremely valuable. It has changed the way I do business. Being a self-employed woman, there are challenges. It was comforting knowing and sharing with other business women, who have experienced the same things where they could give valuable information on their experience and what they did. I have built confidence in myself and how I do business and the results are showing! I have doubled my business in this year. My mentor challenged the way I thought and had me look bigger and to set out what I wanted to achieve in my business, break apart what I could delegate to others and what I needed to do so I didn't burn myself out. Letting go and delegating tasks was a big step; however, a year later, I see how much my business has grown and I am on the path to hitting my goals. If you are looking to grow yourself as a business woman, the mentorship program is a must!

Jacqueline Jeffries, B.Comm

The Womanition Mentorship has been an invaluable experience for me personally, as well as my business. The support of all the mentors has been tremendous and the opportunities presented from the mentorship program have been amazing. I wish the program was longer, and am already thinking of taking it again next year!

Christina Louise Fuchs

I joined the Womanition Mentorship program because I was ready to take my business to the next level and I knew that seeking guidance from women who have been down a similar path was a necessary step in my next level of business. Little did I know that the program would inspire deep reflection both personal and professional.

The result is that I now feel a sense of clarity in where I want to go in my business and how I plan to get there. The best thing was that not only did I have access to my own mentor, but also all the other mentors participating in the program. I found the experience AMAZING, because not only did I learn a lot, but I just genuinely enjoy the company of both the mentees and mentors. I would HIGHLY recommend The Womanition Mentorship program to anyone, especially those women who are ready to put in the work, again both personally and professionally, to rise up in their businesses.

Bianca Osbourne

The Womanition Mentorship Program has been a wonderful experience for me and my business. The program exposes you to even more concepts and people who possess important information that can help a young woman starting out as an entrepreneur succeed. The environment created is full of respect, support, and relationship building since that is at the root of every successful business. Shortly after beginning the program, my business took an unexpected turn and the entire Mentorship group has continued to nurture me and my business in exactly the way it needs. For that I am grateful.

Karli Andreas

I've have been with the Womanition Mentorship Program for 6 months. Womanition has created a program to assist women just like me to enhance and flourish in their businesses. With 30 women all collaborating, you can only imagine the energy in the room that is created. I have gained a world of valuable knowledge and have increased my self-confidence in the business world. My business has been taken in a completely new direction. Womanition has given me the important tools for my "Business toolbox". I highly recommend becoming involved, not only the Mentorship Program, but in Womanition, in general.

Michelle Coates

The mentorship program is a wonderful extension of the Womanition connect group. During the program, I have received a wealth of knowledge from experienced women entrepreneurs. These women understand what you are going through and can provide you with advice and continued support to help you reach your goals. Having my meetings with my mentor has given me the ability to sift through what is working for me and what isn't. I have also been able to put projects in place after brainstorming with my mentor. I would recommend this program to any woman who is in business who may feel like they need some additional support to get to the next level in their business.

Tracy Ness

The Womanition Mentorship program has been inspirational for me. Knowing that there are so many women to lean on as support for me business has been pivotal. My mentor is a strong leader with a generous spirit and I feel very privileged to have had the opportunity to work with her! As a new business, it was extremely helpful when she gave me copies of employee management tools, which allowed me to have a stronger foundation in my hiring, review and letting go process. The tools she gave me will be with me for a long time. I know that her years of expertise in business and gives me the backbone to know that I am making the right decisions for my business. My mentors open hearted communication has allowed me to be myself with her which in turn has allowed my business to continue in a positive direction! Thank you!

Laara Delain

I have been in the Womanition Mentorship program for four months and it has been, at the very least, an eye opening experience. The women who mentor in the program come from a very diverse group. They share a wealth of knowledge, information, and expertise, and are an amazing group of ladies. They have helped me to realize my potential and that anything is possible. These women are wonderful, supportive, and have become a very important part of my personal and business growth. I know that going forward there will always be a great support system for me to build my business and get revitalized both personally and professionally.

Suzzanne Hobson

I considered who I wanted as my mentor before I even signed up to take part in the Womanition mentorship program so when I found out she would be personally mentoring me I was ecstatic! My mentor is an amazing lady who is always trying to help others by give them guidance and strength to succeed in their chosen field. The mentorship program helped me get out of my comfort zone and gave me new confidence in my business. I learned from all the great business leaders — it was great to have so much advice from successful women. I would recommend this program to anyone who is starting out or experienced!

Reena Yost

Thank You for another amazing program. My mentor was the perfect match for me and I learned so much more about business, more than just numbers, what my purpose for the business is, how valuable my time is, and how to set goals to make the best use of it. At every one of the six meetings I took away a list of tools from each mentor and heard a special presentation from each mentor. The various area of expertise from the different mentors covered all aspects of running a business — from marketing to sales to how we show up. As with all your programs – a phenomenal deal and I'm so grateful to be part of Womanition.

Lil Lezarre

MENTORING
WOMEN LEADERS

51348483R00157

Made in the USA
Charleston, SC
16 January 2016